Missing and Exploited Children: Background, Policies, and Issues

Adrienne L. Fernandes-Alcantara
Specialist in Social Policy

February 15, 2013

Congressional Research Service

7-5700

www.crs.gov

RL34050

CRS Report for Congress ———————————————————————

Prepared for Members and Committees of Congress

Summary

Beginning in the late 1970s, highly publicized cases of children abducted, sexually abused, and sometimes murdered prompted policy makers and child advocates to declare a missing children problem. At that time, about 1.5 million children were reported missing annually. Though dated, survey data from 1999 provide the most recent and comprehensive information on missing children. The data show that approximately 1.3 million children went missing from their caretakers that year due to a family or nonfamily abduction, running away or being forced to leave home, becoming lost or injured, or for benign reasons, such as a miscommunication about schedules. Nearly half of all missing children ran away or were forced to leave home, and nearly all missing children were returned to their homes. The number of children who are sexually exploited is unknown because of the secrecy surrounding exploitation; however, in the 1999 study, researchers found that over 300,000 children were victims of rape; unwanted sexual contact; forceful actions taken as part of a sex-related crime; and other sex-related crimes that do not involve physical contact with the child, including those committed on the Internet.

Recognizing the need for greater federal coordination of local and state efforts to recover missing and exploited children, Congress created the Missing and Exploited Children's (MEC) program in 1984 under the Missing Children's Assistance Act (P.L. 98-473, Title IV of the Juvenile Justice and Delinquency Prevention Act of 1974). The act directed the U.S. Department of Justice's Office of Juvenile Justice and Delinquency Prevention (OJJDP) to establish a toll-free number to report missing children and a national resource center for missing and exploited children; coordinate public and private programs to assist missing and exploited children; and provide training and technical assistance to recover missing children.

Since 1984, the National Center for Missing and Exploited Children (NCMEC) has served as the national resource center and has carried out many of the objectives of the act in collaboration with OJJDP. In addition to NCMEC, the MEC program supports (1) the Internet Crimes Against Children (ICAC) Task Force program to assist state and local enforcement cyber units in investigating online child sexual exploitation; (2) training and technical assistance for state AMBER (America's Missing: Broadcast Emergency Response) Alert systems, which publicly broadcast bulletins in the most serious child abduction cases; and (3) other initiatives, including a membership-based nonprofit missing and exploited children's organization that assists families of missing children and efforts to respond to child sexual exploitation through training.

The Missing Children's Assistance Act has been amended multiple times, most recently by the Protecting Our Children Comes First Act (P.L. 110-240). This authorization, which expires at the end of FY2013, outlines the duties of OJJDP and NCMEC in carrying out activities intended to assist missing and exploited children. The ICAC Task Force program is authorized separately under the PROTECT Our Children Act of 2008 (P.L. 110-401), as amended, through FY2018. The AMBER Alert program is authorized under the PROTECT Act (P.L. 108-21). P.L. 108-21 authorized funding for the program in FY2004. Congress has continued to provide funding in each year since then. Missing and exploited children's activities are collectively funded under a single appropriation for the MEC program. For FY2012, Congress appropriated $65 million to the program.

Contents

Figures

Tables

Appendixes

Contacts

Introduction

Beginning in the late 1970s, highly publicized cases of children abducted, sexually abused, and sometimes murdered prompted policy makers and child advocates to declare a missing children problem. At that time, advocates estimated that 1½ million children were reported missing annually, and that some children who went missing were sexually exploited. In some parts of the country, nonprofit organizations formed by the parents of missing children were often the only entities that organized recovery efforts and provided counseling for victimized families.

Recognizing the need for greater federal coordination of local and state efforts to assist missing and exploited children and to publicize information about this population, Congress created the Missing and Exploited Children's (MEC) program in 1984 under the Missing Children's Assistance Act (P.L. 98-473, Title IV of the Juvenile Justice and Delinquency Prevention Act of 1974).[1] The act directed the U.S. Department of Justice's Office of Juvenile Justice and Delinquency Prevention (OJJDP) within the Office of Justice Programs (OJP) to establish both a toll-free number to report missing children and a national resource center and clearinghouse to provide information; coordinate public and private missing and exploited children's programs; and provide training and technical assistance related to missing children. Since 1984, the National Center for Missing and Exploited Children (NCMEC), a nonprofit organization, has carried out these duties in collaboration with OJJDP.

The MEC program supports a range of activities authorized under the Missing Children's Assistance Act and other laws.[2] In addition to NCMEC, the MEC provides funding for (1) the Internet Crimes Against Children (ICAC) Task Force program to assist state and local enforcement cyber units in investigating online child sexual exploitation; (2) training and technical assistance for state AMBER (America's Missing: Broadcast Emergency Response) Alert systems, which publicly broadcast bulletins in the most serious child abduction cases; and (3) other initiatives, including a membership-based nonprofit missing and exploited children's organization that assists families of missing children and efforts to respond to sexual exploitation involving both youth perpetrators and victims. For FY2012, Congress $65 million to the MEC program; FY2013 funding is not yet final. Funding authorization for activities authorized under the Missing Children's Assistance Act expires at the end of FY2013.

This report covers only select aspects of the broader topic of missing and exploited children. It begins with an overview of the scope of the missing and exploited children issue, including definitions and approximate numbers of children known to be missing or exploited. This section also discusses the limitations of data on missing and exploited youth. The report then provides information about the MEC program's funding, oversight, and major components. Finally, the report discusses issues that may be relevant to the MEC program. The end of the report includes

---

[1] The Missing Children's Assistance Act, which outlines the duties of OJDDP and NCMEC, is codified at 42 U.S.C. §5771 et seq. (Chapter 72, Juvenile Justice and Delinquency Prevention). The act was most recently reauthorized by the Protecting Our Children Comes First Act (P.L. 110-240). The ICAC Task Force program is codified at 42 U.S.C. §17601 et seq. (Chapter 154, Combating Child Exploitation) and was authorized under the PROTECT Our Children Act of 2008 (P.L. 110-401), as amended by the Child Protection Act of 2012 (P.L. 112-206). The AMBER Alert program is codified at 42 U.S.C. §5791 (Chapter 72, Juvenile Justice and Delinquency Prevention) and was authorized under the PROTECT Act (P.L. 108-21).

[2] NCMEC coordinates and is involved with several federal activities relating to missing and exploited children. Many of these activities are funded from sources other than the MEC program, although the largest share of federal funds for NCMEC is provided through the program.

---

two appendixes. **Appendix A** provides additional information about the demographics of missing and exploited children and some of the causes and effects of missing and sexual exploitation incidents on victims and families. **Appendix B** presents the major provisions of the Missing Children's Assistance Act of 1984 and amendments to the act.

Demographics of Missing and Exploited Children

Overview

As a policy issue, missing children are often included in discussions of sexual victimization. Missing children and sexually exploited children are distinct but overlapping populations. The term "missing child" is defined under the Missing Children's Assistance Act as an individual under age 18 whose whereabouts are unknown to that individual's legal custodian.[3] Children who go missing—and children who are not missing—may be sexually exploited. Although the act does not define child sexual exploitation, federal statutes, both criminal and civil, specify acts of sexual exploitation for purposes of prosecuting offenders and providing minimum standards of child abuse for states to use in their own definitions of child abuse.

The current number of missing or exploited children is unknown. The Missing Children's Assistance Act requires OJJDP to periodically conduct incidence studies of the number of missing children, the number of children missing due to a stranger abduction or parental abduction, and the number of missing children who are recovered.[4] Since the act's passage in 1984, two national incidence studies, known as the National Incidence Studies of Missing, Abducted, Runaway, and Thrownaway Children (NISMART 1 and 2), have been conducted. However, the studies are dated (one was conducted in 1988 and the other in 1999) and provide limited information about children who were sexually exploited. (Limitations of the data set are discussed in the "Issues" section of this report.)

As discussed below, the 1999 study indicated that of the 1.3 million children who went missing that year, almost half had run away from home or were forced to leave their home, and nearly all were returned to their caretakers. Cases of serious nonfamily abductions, in which the child is transported and held for ransom or killed, were rare. Further, researchers explained that the true number of child sexual exploitation incidents was unknown because of the secrecy around exploitation; however, the study estimated that over 300,000 children were sexually victimized in 1999.

A third national incidence study has been commissioned by OJJDP.[5] As with NISMART-2, the study, known as NISMART-3, will measure the number of stereotypical kidnappings by strangers

---

[3] This definition is codified at 42 U.S.C. §5772. It was changed in 2006 under P.L. 109-248. Previously, the definition included an individual under age 18 whose whereabouts are unknown to that individual's legal custodian if (a) the circumstances surrounding his or her disappearance indicate that the individual may possibly have been removed by another individual from the control of his or her legal custodian without the custodian's consent or (b) the circumstances of the case strongly indicate that the individual is likely to be abused and sexually exploited.

[4] 42 U.S.C. §5773(c).

[5] U.S. Department of Justice, Office of Justice Programs, Office of Juvenile Justice and Delinquency Prevention, Grant Solicitation, *OJJDP FY 2010 National Incidence Studies of Missing, Abducted, Runaway, and Thrownaway Children 3*, 2010, http://ojjdp.ncjrs.gov/grants/solicitations/FY2010/NISMART3.pdf.

and the prevalence of familial abductions; lost, injured, or otherwise missing children; runaway children; and thrownaway children. These figures will be derived from surveys of households, juvenile residential facilities, law enforcement agencies, and other entities that record information on missing child episodes.[6]

Missing Children

NISMART-1

The first national incidence study of missing children, NISMART-1, was conducted in 1988 pursuant to the Missing Children's Assistance Act. NISMART-1 provided the first nationally representative comprehensive data on the incidence of missing children. Unlike previous sources of missing children data, the study provided two counts of children who were missing. One count was based on whether a parent considered the child missing, regardless of the seriousness of the incident, and another was based on whether law enforcement considered a missing child at risk and in need of immediate intervention.[7]

The study classified five categories of missing children: (1) children who were missing because they were lost, injured, or did not adequately communicate with their caretakers about their whereabouts; (2) children abducted by family members; (3) children abducted by non-family members; (4) runaways; and (5) "thrownaways" forced to leave their homes. NISMART-1 did not aggregate the number of missing children across these categories because researchers viewed each category as distinct from other categories. Researchers also raised concerns that some children were not literally missing because caretakers knew of their children's location.

NISMART-2

NISMART-2, conducted in 1999, attempted to resolve some of the methodological challenges of NISMART-1. Based on policy makers' views that missing children (even those not literally missing because their parents knew their whereabouts) share a common experience, data for all missing children were aggregated for "caretaker missing" and "reported missing" cases. For an episode to qualify as "caretaker missing," the child's whereabouts must have been unknown to the primary caretaker, with the result that the caretaker was alarmed for at least one hour and tried to locate the child. In this circumstance, a child could have been missing for benign reasons, such as miscommunication about schedules. A "caretaker missing" child was considered "reported missing" if a caretaker contacted the police or a missing children's agency to locate the child.[8]

---

[6] The NISMART-3 grant was awarded to the Rockville Institute, and funding has been provided in each of FY2010-FY2012. The study continues at present. U.S. Department of Justice, Office of Justice Programs, "Grant Awards by Fiscal Year."

[7] David Finkelhor, Gerald Hotaling, and Andrea J. Sedlak, *Missing, Abducted, Runaway, and Thrownaway Children in America, First Report: Numbers and Characteristics National Incidence Studies*, U.S. Department of Justice, Office of Justice Programs, Office of Juvenile Justice and Delinquency Prevention, May 1990.

[8] Some children reported in NISMART-2 were missing, but their caretakers may not have been alarmed or contacted authorities; these children were identified as "non-missing." See **Appendix A** for a further discussion of non-missing children.

NISMART-2 added to and combined some of the missing children categories created in NISMART-1.[9] "Missing benign" was added as a category to describe a child who goes missing due to a miscommunication and is not in any danger. The survey consolidated the runaway and thrownaway categories that had been separate in NISMART-1. NISMART-2 researchers determined that the categorization of each type of runaway or thrownaway episode frequently depended on whether information was gathered from the children (who tended to emphasize the thrownaway aspects of the episode) or their caretakers (who tended to emphasize the runaway aspects).[10] In short, the categories of missing children include (1) nonfamily abductions; (2) family abductions; (3) missing involuntary, lost, or injured; (4) missing benign; and (5) runaway or thrownaway.[11]

NISMART-2 is the most comprehensive survey to date about missing children. The study relied on a random sample of households and juvenile facilities to develop estimates.[12] Researchers conducted telephone surveys of adults and children in homes, as well as telephone surveys of staff who worked with youth living in juvenile facilities, including shelters for runaway and homeless youth, residential treatment centers, group homes, and youth detention centers. One limitation of the study is that it does not count individuals living in households without telephones or those not living in households, including youth living on the streets and homeless families.

Findings from NISMART-2

NISMART-2 combined the data across the five categories to calculate a total number for both caretaker missing and reported missing episodes. The survey found that 1,315,600 children were missing based on the caretaker missing definition. In about 798,000 (61%) of these cases, parents reported their child missing to the police or a missing children's agency. Nearly all (99.8%) caretaker missing children were recovered. Only 2,500 (0.2%) "caretaker missing" children had not returned home or been located, and the majority of these children were runaways from institutions.[13]

Figure 1 below summarizes the number of caretaker missing and reported missing incidents within the five missing children categories. Children who were missing under multiple categories are included in every category that applies to them. About 36,500 (3%) children experienced more than one type of caretaker missing incident during the year. Therefore, the total number of caretaker missing incidents combined across episodes is 1,352,100. Approximately 31,100 (4%) children experienced more than one type of reported missing incident during the year. Therefore, the total number of reported missing incidents is 828,600.

---

[9] See **Appendix A** for a description of the NISMART-2 missing children categories.

[10] Heather Hammer, David Finkelhor, and Andrea J. Sedlak, *Runaway/Thrownaway Children: National Estimates and Characteristics*, U.S. Department of Justice, Office of Justice Programs, Office of Juvenile Justice and Delinquency Prevention, October 2002, p. 2, http://www.ncjrs.gov/pdffiles1/ojjdp/196469.pdf.

[11] For further information about each of the categories, see **Appendix A**.

[12] NISMART-2 combined data from four sources: the National Household Survey of Adult Caretakers, the National Household Survey of Youth, Law Enforcement Study, and Juvenile Facilities Study. Each sampled child was counted only once in the combined estimate. See Andrea J. Sedlak et al., *National Estimates of Missing Children: An Overview*, U.S. Department of Justice, Office of Justice Programs, Office of Juvenile Justice and Delinquency Prevention, October 2002, p. 5.

[13] Hammer, Finkelhor, and Sedlak, *National Estimates of Missing Children*, p. 6.

Figure 1. Reported Missing and Caretaker Missing, by Missing Category, 1999

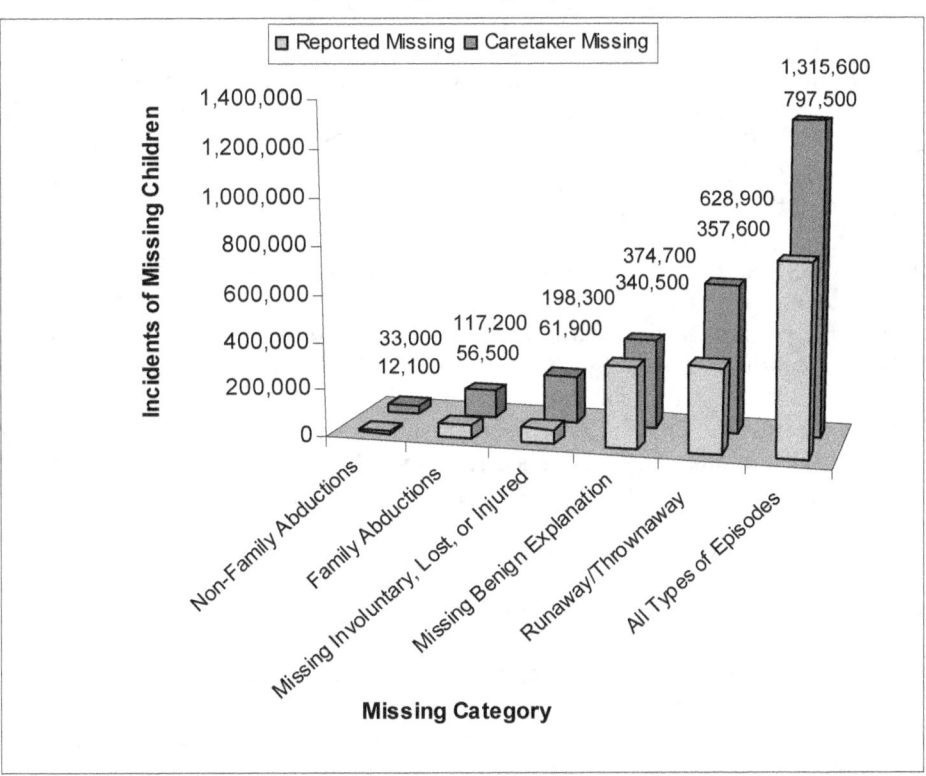

Source: Congressional Research Service presentation of data provided in Table 3 in Andrea J. Sedlak et al., *National Estimates of Missing Children: An Overview*, U.S. Department of Justice, Office of Juvenile Justice and Delinquency Prevention, October 2002, p. 6.

Note: Estimates of caretaker missing children sum to more than the total of 1,315,600 because 36,500 (3%) children who experienced multiple episodes are included in every category that applies to them, but these multiple counts are not included in the total. Estimates of reported missing children sum to more than the total of 797,500 because 31,100 (4%) children who experienced multiple episodes are included in every category that applies to them, but these multiple counts also are not included in the total.

Nearly half of the caretaker missing children and 45% of the reported missing children in NISMART-2 had run away or were forced to leave their homes.[14] Children missing due to benign reasons comprised the next largest share in both categories: 28% in the caretaker missing category and 43% in the reported missing category. Family abductions made up 9% of the caretaker missing children population and 7% of the reported missing children population. Finally, nonfamily abductions comprised 3% of caretaker missing children and 2% of reported missing children.

Stereotypical kidnapping—in which a stranger or slight acquaintance detained the child overnight, traveled at least 50 miles, and held the child for ransom or killed the child—is a type of nonfamily abduction. Extensive media coverage about stereotypical kidnapping cases, such as those involving Adam Walsh (1981), Polly Klaas (1993), and Elizabeth Smart (2002), may

---

[14] Sedlak et al., *National Estimates of Missing Children*, p. 7.

contribute to the belief that these missing children incidents are common. However, such cases are rare. With the caveat that NISMART-2 data on stereotypical kidnappings are not entirely reliable because estimates are based on too few sample cases, about 90 of the reported missing nonfamily abduction victims in 1999 experienced a stereotypical kidnapping (this information is not shown in **Figure 1**).[15] Although nonfamily abductions rarely result in more serious cases, children who are not recovered immediately in such cases are at increased risk of becoming harmed. Studies show that the first three hours after an abduction are the most crucial for the recovery of the child. Just over three-quarters of abducted children who are murdered are dead within three hours of the abduction.[16]

NISMART-2 shows that the children missing tended to be teenagers, male, and white. About half (45% of caretaker missing and 44% of reported missing) of missing children were between the ages of 15 and 17. The next largest share of children (31% and 30%) were between the ages of 12 and 14 in both categories, followed by children ages 6 to 11 (13% and 14%) and children 0 to 5 (11% and 12%). A majority of the children were male—57% of the caretaker missing children and 51% of the reported missing children. Though whites made up the greatest proportion (57% and 54%) of missing children, they were underrepresented compared to their share of the total U.S. population; black (16% and 19%) and Hispanic (18% and 21%) children were overrepresented.

Defining Child Sexual Exploitation

Child sexual exploitation generally refers to the use of a child for the sexual gratification of an adult, and a child can be exploited regardless of whether he or she goes missing.[17] This exploitation includes a continuum of exploitation ranging from child sexual molestation to the production of child pornography and trafficking of children for sexual purposes. Both Title 18 (Crimes and Criminal Procedure) and Title 42 (Public Health and Welfare) of the U.S. Code address sexually exploitative acts involving children.

Title 18 prohibits the following crimes involving the sexual exploitation of children: commerce in child pornography;[18] crossing state lines to engage in a sexual act with a child; engaging in child prostitution and child sex trafficking across state lines; transferring obscene material to a child by mail or through interstate or foreign travel; traveling abroad to engage in a sexual act with a child; and using a misleading domain name, words, or digital images on the Internet with the intent to

---

[15] David Finkelhor, Heather Hammer, and Andrea J. Sedlak, *Nonfamily Abducted Children: National Estimates and Characteristics*, U.S. Department of Justice, Office of Justice Programs, Office of Juvenile Justice and Delinquency Prevention, October 2002, p. 6, http://www.ncjrs.gov/pdffiles1/ojjdp/196467.pdf. (Hereinafter referred to as Finkelhor, Hammer, Sedlak, *Nonfamily Abducted Children*.)

[16] Katherine M. Brown et al. *Case Management for Missing Children Homicide Investigation*, Office of the Attorney General, State of Washington and U.S. Department of Justice, Office of Justice Programs, Office of Juvenile Justice and Delinquency Prevention, May 2006, p. 13, http://www.missingkids.com/en_US/documents/homicide_missing.pdf.

[17] David Finkelhor et al., *A Sourcebook on Child Sexual Abuse* (Beverly Hills: Sage Publications, 1984), pp. 22-27 and Richard J. Estes, *The Sexual Exploitation of Children: A Working Guide to the Empirical Literature*, August 2001, p. 6.

[18] This includes possessing, receiving, reproducing, distributing, and advertising to receive, trade, buy, or distribute child pornography. It also extends to a parent or guardian who permits a minor to produce a visual depiction of sexually explicit conduct. Notably, federal courts have upheld the constitutionality of federal child pornography statutes that criminalize intrastate possession by finding the activity sufficiently connected to Congress's broader scheme of regulating the interstate commercial market for child pornography. For further information, see CRS Report RL30315, *Federalism, State Sovereignty, and the Constitution: Basis and Limits of Congressional Power*, by Kenneth R. Thomas.

---

deceive a minor into viewing material that is harmful to that minor.[19] As discussed below, NCMEC fields reports of sexual crimes against children through its CyberTipline, which includes eight categories that are mostly based on these federal criminal statutes. In addition, state and local law enforcement agencies have the authority to investigate these crimes because child sexual exploitation is generally outlawed in all 50 states and the District of Columbia.[20]

Title 42 provides two types of definitions related to child sexual exploitation. First, 42 U.S.C. Section 5101g, as enacted by the Child Abuse Prevention and Treatment Act (CAPTA, as amended), provides the minimum standards of child abuse—including child sexual abuse—that states must incorporate into their statutory definitions of child abuse and neglect in order to be eligible to receive funding under CAPTA.[21] According to CAPTA, the term "sexual abuse" includes "(1) the employment, use, persuasion, inducement, enticement, or coercion of any child to engage in, or to assist any other person to engage in, any sexually explicit conduct or simulation of such conduct for the purpose of producing a visual depiction of such conduct; or (2) the rape, and in cases of inter-familial relationships, statutory rape, molestation, prostitution, or other form of sexual exploitation of children, or incest with children." Guardians of children under age 18 who are investigated for engaging in these acts or failing to adequately protect their children from such acts may be penalized under state civil and criminal procedures governing child abuse and neglect.

Second, specified crimes of sexual exploitation are defined under 42 U.S.C. Section 16911, as enacted by the Adam Walsh Child Protection and Safety Act of 2006 (P.L. 109-248).The law modified federal guidelines for state programs that require individuals convicted of crimes against children or sexually violent crimes to register his or her address.[22] Specified crimes of sexual exploitation requiring offender registration include criminal sexual conduct against a minor; solicitation of a minor to engage in sexual conduct; use of a minor in a sexual performance; solicitation of a minor to practice prostitution; video voyeurism (such as watching a child on a web-cam); possession, production, manufacture, and distribution of child pornography; criminal sexual conduct involving a minor or the use of the Internet to facilitate or attempt such conduct; and any conduct that by its nature is a sex offense against a minor.

Incidents of Child Sexual Exploitation

The true number of sexual exploitation incidents—whether they accompany missing children cases or not—is unknown because this type of abuse often goes undetected. In addition, studies of child sexual exploitation report varying numbers because of differences in their methodology, the time periods in which the data were collected, and differences in how exploitation is defined.

---

[19] Most federal criminal statutes on child sexual exploitation are in Chapters 71, 77, 109A, 109B, 110, and 117 of Title 18 of the U.S. Code. For further information about select offenses, see CRS Report R42132, *Sexual Abuse of Children: Federal Criminal Offenses*, by Richard M. Thompson II.

[20] National District Attorneys Association, National Center for Prosecution of Child Abuse, "NCPCA State Statues," http://www.ndaa.org/ncpca_state_statutes.html. See statues pertaining to child pornography, prostitution of children, child protection, sexual offenses, and trafficking.

[21] U.S. Department of Health and Human Services, Child Welfare Information Gateway, *Definitions of Child Abuse and Neglect: Summary of State Laws*, http://www.childwelfare.gov/systemwide/laws_policies/statutes/define.pdf.

[22] This program was originally created under the Jacob Wetterling Crimes Against Children Act and Sexually Violent Offender Registration Act, codified at 42 U.S.C. §14701 (Title XVII of the Violent Crime Control and Law Enforcement Act of 1994, P.L. 103-322).

Nonetheless, three sources—NISMART-2, the National Survey of Children's Exposure to Violence, and data collected by NCMEC—provide some insight into the prevalence of sexual exploitation.[23] In short, the data show that a significant number and share of children under age 18 have been sexually victimized.

NISMART-2

In addition to asking questions about children going missing, NISMART-2 surveyed a representative sample of children under age 18 and their caretakers about whether children were victims of sexual exploitation. The study found that in 1999 approximately 285,400 children were victims of sexual assault, which encompasses unwanted sexual conduct involving the use of force or threat.[24] Examples of sexual assault include rape, unwanted sexual conduct when the perpetrator touches the child's private parts, or when the child is forced or coerced to touch the perpetrator's private parts. An additional 35,000 children were victims of other sex offenses that did not involve physical contact or force, primarily acts of exhibitionism or voyeurism. In total, more than 300,000 children were believed to have been sexually victimized in 1999.

National Survey of Children's Exposure to Violence

The National Survey of Children's Exposure to Violence, conducted by the University of New Hampshire with support from OJJDP, examines the incidence and prevalence of children's exposure to violence.[25] Researchers interviewed a nationally representative sample of children under age 18 and their caretakers by phone. They asked whether children had experienced certain forms of violence and victimization, including sexual victimization, within the past year and over their lifetime. The sexual victimization category encompasses seven types of victimization: sexual conduct or fondling by an adult the child knew, sexual conduct or fondling by an adult stranger, sexual contact or fondling by another child or teenager, attempted or completed intercourse, exposure or "flashing," sexual harassment, and consensual sexual conduct with an adult. The study found that 1 in 16 (6.1%) surveyed children and youth were sexually victimized in the past year and nearly 1 in 10 (9.8%) were sexually victimized over their lifetimes. Girls were more likely than boys to report that they had been sexually victimized, with 7.4% of girls reporting sexual victimization within the past year and 12.2% reporting victimization over their lifetimes. Female adolescents ages 14 to 17 had the highest rate of victimization. Nearly 8% had been sexually victimized within the past year and 18.7% had been sexually victimized over their lifetimes.

---

[23] Researchers have provided estimates of the number of children in the child welfare system who were sexually exploited and the number of children at risk of sexual exploitation via the Internet and commercial sexual exploitation (see **Appendix A** for information about these studies).

[24] David Finkelhor, Heather Hammer, and Andrea J. Sedlak, *Sexually Assaulted Children: National Estimates and Characteristics*, U.S. Department of Justice, Office of Justice Programs, Office of Juvenile Justice and Delinquency Prevention, August 2008; http://www.ncjrs.gov/pdffiles1/ojjdp/214383.pdf.

[25] David Finkelhor et al., *Children's Exposure to Violence: A Comprehensive National Survey*, U.S. Department of Justice, Office of Justice Programs, Office of Juvenile Justice and Delinquency Prevention, October 2009, http://www.ncjrs.gov/pdffiles1/ojjdp/227744.pdf.

Incidents Reported to the NCMEC CyberTipline

One measure of the prevalence of child sexual exploitation is the number of incidents reported to NCMEC's CyberTipline. The CyberTipline began in March 1998 to serve 24 hours a day, seven days a week as the national clearinghouse for tips and leads about child sexual exploitation.[26] As required under statute, the tipline allows individuals and electronic communication service providers (ESPs) to report incidents under eight categories: (1) possession, manufacture, and distribution of child pornography; (2) online enticement of children for sexual acts; (3) child prostitution; (4) child sex tourism; (5) child sexual molestation (not in the family); (6) unsolicited obscene material sent to a child; (7) misleading domain names; and (8) misleading words or digital images on the Internet. These reports are forwarded to ICAC task forces and other law enforcement officials for investigation. In FY2011, the CyberTipline received 277,552 reports of child sexual exploitation, most of which (96.3%) were submitted in the category of child pornography.[27]

Description and Funding of the Missing and Exploited Children's (MEC) Program

Overview

The MEC program is the centerpiece of federal efforts to prevent the abduction and exploitation of children and to recover those children who do go missing. The program was created by the Missing Children's Assistance Act of 1984 in response to increasing concern about the abduction and sexual exploitation of children in the late 1970s and early 1980s.[28] At that time, many of the victims' families and communities perceived that kidnappings were becoming more commonplace. Prominent cases of missing children were highly publicized and a docudrama, "Adam," depicted the story of abducted six-year-old Adam Walsh, son of John and Revé Walsh.[29]

Testimony at congressional hearings about missing children further reinforced the perception of a missing children problem. Witnesses testified that as many as 1.8 million children were missing. They also highlighted the accompanying sexual exploitation that children often experienced during missing episodes. Senator Mitch McConnell, then chairman of the Kentucky Task Force on Exploited and Missing Children, said that the nexus between exploited and missing children was evident by the fact that nearly 10% of 844 missing children in one Kentucky county were

---

[26] NCMEC's role as administrator of the CyberTipline was authorized by the Prosecutorial Remedies and Other Tools to End the Exploitation of Children Today (PROTECT) Act of 2003 (P.L. 108-21).

[27] NCMEC, *NCMEC Quarterly Progress Reports for October 1, 2010 Through September 30, 2011.*

[28] The Missing Children Act of 1982 (P.L. 97-292) was the first piece of legislation related to missing children. The legislation added one new section to existing law (at the time) that directed the Attorney General to keep records on missing children in the National Crime Information Center's (FBI) Missing Persons File and to disseminate those records to state and local agencies. That law neither created new federal jurisdiction over missing children's programs nor required federal law enforcement officials to coordinate missing children efforts.

[29] Martin L. Forst and Martha-Elin Blomquist, *Missing Children* (New York: Lexington Books, 1991), pp. 56-66.

---

sexually exploited.[30] Hearings on the act also underscored the need for the federal government to coordinate efforts to locate missing children and prosecute their abductors. McConnell testified:

> Communities such as mine and states such as Kentucky are attempting to do all that they can to assist missing children and better protect all children from exploitation and abuse. There is a point, however, beyond which we cannot go and where our resources cannot reach. [A national missing children program] picks up where our work leaves off and will go a long way toward plugging the holes and gaps in the system.

The Missing Children's Assistance Act was passed shortly thereafter to address concerns about coordination and to direct the Department of Justice's Office of Juvenile Justice and Delinquency Prevention (OJJDP) Administrator to lead federal efforts to recover missing children through the MEC program. The legislation established a national resource center and clearinghouse designed to provide technical assistance to state and local governments and law enforcement agencies, as well as disseminate information about the national incidence of missing children. Further, the OJJDP Administrator was directed to establish a toll-free telephone line to report information about missing children.

The Missing Children's Assistance Act has been amended multiple times since 1984. Major amendments include (1) requiring OJJDP to disseminate information about free or low-cost legal, restaurant, lodging, and transportation services to families of missing children (P.L. 100-690); (2) formalizing NCMEC's role as the nation's clearinghouse for missing and exploited children and authorizing separate funding levels for NCMEC (P.L. 106-71); (3) formalizing NCMEC's role in overseeing activities to track reports of online child sexual exploitation (P.L. 108-21); and (4) codifying and expanding many of the activities already carried out by NCMEC (P.L. 110-240). **Appendix B** provides a description of the original act and its amendments.

The MEC program also provides funding for activities authorized under separate laws. The ICAC Task Force program was authorized under the PROTECT Our Children Act of 2008 (P.L. 110-401) and the AMBER Alert program was authorized under the PROTECT Act (P.L. 108-21).

Administration and Funding

The Child Protection Division in the Department of Justice's Office of Juvenile Justice and Delinquency Prevention (under the Office of Justice Programs) administers the MEC program. NCMEC has served as the national resource center and clearinghouse since 1984.

The MEC program was first funded at $4 million in FY1985 and has steadily received funding increases in all subsequent years beginning in 1991, except in FY1994 through FY1997, FY2011, and FY2012. Funding more than doubled from $6 million in FY1997 to $12.3 million in FY1998, when the ICAC Task Force program was implemented. Another funding peak, from FY2004 to FY2005, was the result of increased funds for NCMEC. Funding increased again—from $50 million in FY2008 to $70 million—in FY2009, the year following the most recent reauthorization of the program. Also in FY2009, Congress appropriated funding for the program under the American Recovery and Reinvestment Act (P.L. 111-5). ARRA provides funding for myriad

---

[30] Testimony of Mitch McConnell, in U.S. Congress, Senate Committee on the Judiciary, Subcommittee on Juvenile Justice, *Missing Children's Assistance Act* hearing, 98th Congress, 2nd sess., February 7, 1984 (Washington: GPO, 1984).

federal programs and initiatives to address the economic recession that began in December 2007 and extended through June 2009. The law appropriated $50 million for the ICAC Task Force program. The funds supported four grant programs authorized under P.L. 110-401: (1) ICAC grants, which were awarded on a formula basis (as required by the law) and other criteria to existing task forces; (2) ICAC Training and Technical Assistance grants, which provide training to ICAC task forces and other law enforcement agencies in the areas of investigation, forensics, and prosecution, among other topics; (3) ICAC Research grants to encourage innovative and independent research and data collection to further understand the scope and prevalence of technology and Internet crimes against children; and (4) the National ICAC Data System, which is intended to provide a secure, dynamic undercover infrastructure to facilitate online law enforcement investigations of child exploitation, among other purposes.[31]

Table 1 shows the total funding and funding for each of the components from FY2004 through FY2012, and estimated funding for FY2013. NCMEC has received the most funding in each year, followed by the ICAC Task Force program. In some years, the AMBER Alert program has received the next highest level of funding, followed by funding for other activities. These activities include program administration, support services for missing children's organizations, and grant programs that can vary from year to year. For example, FY2011 funds supported grants for conferences focusing on missing and exploited children and an organization to provide technical assistance to OJJDP grantees and other organizations addressing commercial sexual exploitation and sex trafficking of children.

FY2012 Funding

After passing two temporary spending measures (P.L. 112-33 and P.L. 112-36), Congress appropriated $65 million to the MEC program in FY2012 under the Consolidated and Further Continuing Appropriations Act, 2012 (P.L. 112-55). This represents a reduction of about 7% from the program's funding of $69.8 million in FY2011. The conference report to accompany P.L. 112-55 specified that funding for the program should be used "to continue to expand efforts to protect the Nation's children, focusing on the areas of locating missing children, and addressing the growing wave of child sexual exploitation facilitated by the Internet.... The conferees are aware that one way OJP addresses the proliferation of Internet crimes against children is through ICAC task forces. With regard to ICAC task forces, the conferees encourage the Department to fund programs with proven training results and low administrative costs."[32]

The Obama Administration proposed funding the Missing and Exploited Children's program at $60 million for FY2012.[33] According to the Administration, this decrease was proposed as part of the overall goal of reducing the federal deficit.

---

[31] Funds were awarded for three of the grants in FY2009: ICAC Grants ($41.5 million); ICAC Training and Technical Assistance Grants ($5.1 million to six organizations); and ICAC Research Grants ($2.0 million to the University of Hawaii and University of New Hampshire). Funding was awarded for the National ICAC Data System Grant in FY2010 ($.9 million to the Massachusetts State Police). U.S. Department of Justice, Office of Justice Programs," "Funding," http://www.ojp.usdoj.gov/funding/funding.htm. See the "Internet Crimes Against Children (ICAC) Task Force" section for further information on the National ICAC Data System. An additional $487,556 was handled by the National Institute of Justice to complete an evaluation of ICAC Community Education programs.

[32] U.S. Congress, *Conference Report to Accompany H.R. 2112, Consolidated and Further Continuing Appropriations Act, 2012*, 112th Cong., 1st sess., 2011, H.Rept. 112-284.

[33] U.S. Department of Justice, Office of Justice Programs, *FY2012 Performance Budget*, p. 241, http://www.justice.gov/jmd/2012justification/pdf/fy12-ojp-justification.pdf.

FY2013 Funding

On September 28, 2012, President Obama signed the Continuing Appropriations Resolution, 2013 (P.L. 112-175) to provide FY2013 appropriations through March 27, 2013. The extension generally provides an increase of 0.612% over the FY2012 level for most discretionary programs, including the missing and exploited children's program. The law was not accompanied by a conference report or explanatory statement that indicated exact appropriation amounts by program. As of mid-January 2013, DOJ had not yet published information about the FY2013 budget under the CR.

As part of the FY2013 budget request, the Department of Justice proposed funding the MEC program at $67 million through a transfer from the Crime Victims Fund (CVF) to the State and Local Law Enforcement Assistance account within the Office of Justice Programs. The CVF is administered by OJP's Office for Victims of Crime (OVC) and does not receive appropriated funding. Deposits to the CVF come from criminal fines, forfeited bail bonds, penalties, and special assessments collected by the U.S. Attorneys' Offices, federal U.S. courts, and the Federal Bureau of Prisons from offenders convicted of federal crimes.[34] Under this proposal, the MEC program would continue to be administered through OJP's Office of Juvenile Justice and Delinquency Prevention. DOJ did not propose how funding within the MEC program should be allocated in FY2013.[35]

---

[34] For further information, see archived CRS Report RL32579, *Victims of Crime Compensation and Assistance: Background and Funding.*

[35] U.S. Department of Justice, *Office of Justice Programs, FY2013 Performance Budget,* http://www.justice.gov/jmd/ 2013justification/pdf/fy13-ojp-justification.pdf.

Table 1. Actual Funding for the Missing and Exploited Children's Program by Component, FY2004 to FY2012, Plus Funding Under the American Recovery and Reinvestment Act (ARRA, P.L. 111-5)

($ in millions)

Program Component	FY2004[a]	FY2005[a]	FY2006[a]	FY2007[a]	FY2008	FY2009	ARRA	FY2010	FY2011[a]	FY2012
NCMEC	$17.8	$26.6	$26.6	$26.5	$26.3	30.5	N/A	30.5	$30.1	$32.2
ICAC Task Force Program[b]	12.4	13.3	14.3	14.3[c]	16.9	25.0	$50.0[d]	30.0	$30.0	$25.7
AMBER Alert Training and Technical Assistance	4.0	4.9	4.9	5.0	4.8	5.0	N/A	4.0	4.1	2.5
Other Missing and Exploited Children's Activities[e]	1.5	1.5	1.5	1.7	2.0	9.5	N/A	5.5	5.6	3.6
MEC Program Total Funding	$35.7	$46.3	$47.4	$47.5	$50.0	$70.0	$50.0	$70.0	$69.8	$65.0

Source: Congressional Research Service, based on information provided by the U.S. Department of Justice, Office of Justice Programs, May 2007, September 2008, June 2009, January 2010, March, April, and December 2011; U.S. Department of Justice, *Office of Justice Programs, FY2011 Performance Budget*, p. 54; U.S. Department of Justice, *Office of Justice Programs, FY2012 Performance Budget*, p. 241; Department of Defense and Full-Year Continuing Appropriations Act, 2011 (P.L. 112-10); the Consolidated and Further Continuing Appropriations Act, 2012 (P.L. 112-55); Continuing Appropriations Resolution, 2013 (P.L. 112-175).

Notes: N/A means not applicable. The Missing Children's Assistance Act, as amended by the Protecting Our Children Comes First Act of 2007 (P.L. 110-240), authorizes funding for NCMEC at $40 million annually for FY2008 and such sums as necessary for FY2009-FY2013 (42 U.S.C. 5773(b)(2). The act also authorizes such sums as necessary for other activities carried out by DOJ for FY2009 through FY2013 (42 U.S.C. 5777). The PROTECT Our Children Act of 2008 (P.L. 110-401) provides two authorizations for the ICAC Task Force program—one for $2 million for each of FY2009-FY2016 to collect and report data (42 U.S.C. §17615(h) and one for $60 million for FY2009-FY2013 for other ICAC activities, including grants for ICAC task forces (42 U.S.C. §17617). The Child Protection Act of 2012 (P.L. 112-240) extended authorization for ICAC activities through FY2018, including ICAC task forces. The PROTECT Act (P.L. 108-21) provides two authorizations for the AMBER Alert program—one for $10 million for FY2004 only (to DOJ) to assist states develop and implement their respective AMBER Alert programs (42 U.S.C. §5791(c)(f)) and $20 million for FY2004 only (to the Department of Transportation) for states to develop and enhance communications systems along highways for alerts.

a. FY2004 through FY2006 reflect appropriations less rescissions. The FY2007 appropriation is based on the FY2006 funding level minus 0.02%. The FY2011 appropriation is based on the FY2010 funding level minus 0.02%.

b. Funds for the ICAC program include funding for training and technical assistance and research.

c. The ICAC Task Force Program received an additional $11.5 million in 2007 through the Byrne Discretionary Grant Program to expand the program, provide training and technical assistance, and improve the forensic capabilities of and reduce the backlog of cases handled by the task forces. These funds are not included in this table.

d. The ICAC funding received under ARRA supported four ICAC activities authorized under the PROTECT Our Children Act of 2008 (P.L. 110-401): (1) ICAC grants; (2) ICAC Training and Technical Assistance grant; (3) ICAC Research grants to encourage innovative and independent research and data collection to further understand the scope and prevalence of technology and Internet crimes against children; and (4) the National ICAC Data System.

e. Includes funding for program administration, support services for missing children's organizations, and grant programs that can vary from year to year. For example, FY2011 funds supported grants for conferences focusing on missing and exploited children and an organization to provide technical assistance to OJJDP grantees and other organizations addressing commercial sexual exploitation and sex trafficking of children.

The remainder of this report discusses the components of the MEC program and issues for Congress.

National Center for Missing and Exploited Children

NCMEC is a primary component of the MEC program and employs more than 300 employees at its Alexandria, VA, headquarters and regional offices in California, Florida, New York, and Texas. These regional offices provide case management and technical support in their geographic areas.

NCMEC provides multiple activities and services pertaining to (1) missing children, including those abducted to or from the United States; (2) exploited children; (3) training and technical assistance; (4) families of missing children; and (5) partnerships with state clearinghouses, the private sector, and children's organizations. These activities and services are detailed below.[36] Note that some missing children and exploited children programs are not mutually exclusive and that this report does not provide an exhaustive discussion of all services provided by NCMEC.

In addition to funding through the MEC program, NCMEC is also funded through contributions and the United States Secret Service (USSS) in the Department of Homeland Security. Pursuant to the Violent Crime and Law Enforcement Act of 1994 (P.L. 103-322), Congress has mandated that the USSS provide forensic and technical assistance to NCMEC and federal, state, and local law enforcement agencies in matters involving missing and exploited children.

Missing Children's Services

Call Center

NCMEC's Call Center receives calls on its 24-hour, national and international toll-free hotline (1-800-THE-LOST) primarily from parents and law enforcement officials. From October 1984 through the end of FY2012, the Center handled nearly 3.7 million calls with reports on missing children; sightings of missing children; and requests for assistance, information, and technical assistance from families of missing children, law enforcement agencies, and others.[37] Calls for services involving missing-children cases ("case" labels are based on one or more children and do not represent a single incident), leads or sightings of missing children, requests for information and assistance, and (since 1987) reports of child exploitation through the Child Pornography Tipline (now known as the CyberTipline), are routed to the Call Center.[38] Call Center staff assist law enforcement and other professionals in cases of missing and exploited children and transfer call data regarding runaway children to the National Runaway Switchboard (1-800-RUNAWAY). Assistance activities range from sending publications or educational materials to providing

---

[36] Unless otherwise noted, the description of these services is based on a site visit to NCMEC, interviews and ongoing correspondence with NCMEC staff, and quarterly progress reports submitted by NCMEC to the Department of Justice about the status of the grant received under the Missing and Exploited Children's program.

[37] NCMEC, *NCMEC Quarterly Progress Report: October 1-December 31, 2012*, p. 5.

[38] Calls on the Child Pornography Tipline are taken on behalf of the U.S. Department of Homeland Security's Immigration and Customs Enforcement; U.S. Postal Inspection Service; Federal Bureau of Investigation; and U.S. Secret Service, and include victims of pornography, prostitution, sex rings, and sex tourism. This reflects activity since June 1987.

technical support to law enforcement and families about missing children cases. The Call Center also provides information to families of missing children about free or low-cost transportation services or requests transportation for families needing assistance with reunification. NCMEC partners with American Airlines, Continental Airlines, Amtrak, and Greyhound to transport families.

NCMEC is the only nonprofit, non-law enforcement entity to have access to the FBI's National Crime Information Center's (NCIC) Missing Person File,[39] which is reviewed by Call Center staff for records of missing children added by local and state law enforcement agencies and updates of these records. The Crime Control Act of 1990 (P.L. 101-647) requires law enforcement agencies that enter cases into the NCIC database to work with NCMEC to receive information and technical support. Cases of children who are believed to be seriously at risk are flagged in NCIC for NCMEC. NCMEC is permitted to search the Missing Person File for adult missing person cases because some missing children, upon reaching the age of majority, are reentered into NCIC as missing adults.

Case Management

Each missing child case is entered into NCMEC's nationwide database and a case manager in the Missing Children's Division is assigned. NCMEC case managers serve as the single point of contact for the searching family and provide technical assistance to locate abductors and recover missing children.

In FY2012, case managers handled nearly 11,000 cases (i.e., individual children). About eight out of ten (81.1%) of the cases involved endangered runaways, followed by victims of family abduction.[40]

Project ALERT (America's Law Enforcement Retiree Team)

The Project ALERT program was established in 1992 to assist law enforcement agencies with the recovery of missing children at no cost to the agencies. Project ALERT members include 173 retired federal, state, and local law enforcement officials who have recent and relevant investigative experience and complete a 40-hour certification course.[41] Project ALERT services include case review, organization, recommendation of investigative strategies, assistance with case interviews, and liaison efforts with the family of a missing child. Representatives also conduct outreach to the community through public speaking and attending conferences.

---

[39] The NCIC is a computerized index of information on crimes and criminals that is maintained by the Federal Bureau of Investigation (FBI). NCIC data are reported by federal, state, and local law enforcement officials. The FBI authorizes the National Central Bureau of Interpol to input missing-child cases into the Missing Person File where no U.S. law enforcement agency jurisdiction exists (42 U.S.C. §5780). For additional information about the NCIC, see U.S. Department of Justice, Federal Bureau of Investigation (FBI), *National Crime Information Center*, http://www.fbi.gov/about-us/cjis/ncic/ncic.

[40] NCMEC, *NCMEC Quarterly Progress Reports, July 1, 2012-September 30, 2012*, p 9.

[41] Ibid, p. 16.

Team Adam

Team Adam, created in 2003, is a rapid, on-site response and support system that provides no-cost investigative and technical assistance to local law enforcement officers. The team is staffed by 84 retired federal, state, and local investigators chosen by a committee with representatives from the FBI and state and local law enforcement executives experienced in crimes-against-children investigations.[42] Team Adam consultants determine, through contact with the law enforcement agency and the victim's family, which additional resources or assistance would be valuable with the search for the victim, the investigation of the crime, and family crisis management.

Forensic Services Unit

The Forensic Services Unit is composed of the Forensic Imaging Unit, Cold Case Unit, and Unidentified Victims Unit; the teams assist in the recovery of long-term missing children and work to identify the remains of children and young adults believed to have gone missing.

Forensic Imaging Unit

The Forensic Imaging Unit was created in 1990 to age-progress images of missing children. The unit's technicians age-progress photos of children through software programs using the most recent picture of the child. The image is stretched to approximate normal cranial and facial growth, and the stretched image is merged and blended with a photograph of an immediate biological family member.[43] The age-progressed image appears in clothing and a hairstyle consistent with the child's current age. Missing children photos are age-progressed every two years and adult photos are age-progressed in five-year increments. Age-progressed images are distributed to the local police, searching families, media, and posted on the NCMEC website.

Age-regressed images are also created by the forensic unit. These images are produced at the request of law enforcement agents posing as youth in online communication with adults who seek to engage in sexual acts with children. Agents in their twenties and thirties (usually) send their photograph to NCMEC, and they are made to appear as adolescents. Finally, the age-progression unit creates facial and skull reconstructions of missing children based on recovered remains. The unit works with an offsite forensic anthropologist who CAT-scans the remains. Based on the digital depiction of the image and discussions with the anthropologist about the child's likely background (race, gender, age), the unit creates a black-and-white digital profile (so as to not provide exact eye/hair/skin tones) of the child. The Forensic Imaging Unit might also reference medical examiner records and newspaper clippings from the area where the child was recovered.

Cold Case Unit and Unidentified Victims Unit[44]

Analysts in these units provide support and resources to the "cold" cases of long-term missing children and cases of unidentified human remains of victims believed to be children and young

---

[42] Ibid, p. 17.

[43] NCMEC, *Forensic Imaging Activities*. This description of forensic imaging activities is from an internal document made available to CRS by NCMEC in March 2007.

[44] National Center for Missing and Exploited Children, *2009 Annual Report*, http://www.missingkids.com/en_US/publications/NC171.pdf.

adults. They also assist law enforcement and medical examiners/coroners in cases of child homicides and identification. NCMEC has partnered with the University of North Texas to offer parents and family members of missing children an opportunity to have their DNA samples profiled and uploaded to the FBI's Combined DNA Index System (CODIS), where once a week, the DNA of the missing child is scanned against the DNA profiles of unidentified persons.

International Missing Children's Cases[45]

NCMEC assists with cases of children abducted to and from the United States. From 1995 through May 2008, NCMEC had a Cooperative Agreement with the State Department and OJJDP, to handle *incoming* cases of international abduction cases under The Hague Convention on the Civil Aspects of International Child Abduction (the "Hague Convention").[46] The State Department is now responsible for handling these cases. NCMEC assists the State Department with developing and distributing posters for missing children abducted to the United States. Signatories to the Convention pledge to work toward the prompt return of abducted children. Of the 192 formally recognized countries in the world, however, 126 lack formal civil mechanisms in place with the United States to facilitate the return of a parentally abducted child.[47]

NCMEC also coordinates cases of American children abducted abroad, or *outgoing* cases. NCMEC provides technical assistance to law enforcement via the International Parental Kidnapping Crime Act (P.L. 103-173), which criminalizes removing a child from the United States "with the intent to obstruct the lawful exercise of parental rights."[48]

NCMEC handles hundreds of prevention and abduction-in-progress matters each year that involve international abduction. NCMEC also coordinates the provision of pro-bono legal assistance to victim families and provides technical support, including legal technical assistance to parents, lawyers, court officers, law enforcement officials, and others.

Exploited Children's Division

Pursuant to the Violent Crime and Law Enforcement Act of 1994 (P.L. 103-322), Congress mandated that the United States Secret Service (USSS) provide forensic and technical assistance to NCMEC and federal, state, and local law enforcement agencies in matters involving missing and exploited children. NCMEC's Exploited Children's Division was established in January 1997 with a grant from USSS received pursuant to P.L. 103-322.

---

[45] The International Centre for Missing and Exploited Children ("ICMEC") is a sister organization affiliated with NCMEC. ICMEC focuses on policy, advocacy, and training, and does not perform case work. ICMEC advocates for adoption of treaties in regards to children's rights; engages international law enforcement officials, civil service organizations, and government representatives; offers technical assistance in creating missing children centers; and creates and distributes reports on international child abduction and child sexual exploitation.

[46] The Department of State is designated as the U.S. Central Authority for the Hague Convention. NCMEC was permitted to serve as the representative of the State Department pursuant to 42 U.S.C. §11608.

[47] NCMEC, *NCMEC Quarterly Progress Report: July 1-September 30, 2012*, p. 55, footnote 56.

[48] The term parental rights refers to the right to joint or sole physical custody of a child obtained through a court order, a legally binding agreement between the involved parties, or by operation of law. For further information about the International Parental Kidnapping Crime Act and the Hague Convention, see CRS Report RS21261, *International Parental Child Abductions*, by Alison M. Smith.

The ECD administers the Child Victim ID Program (CVIP) and CyberTipline. The unit also analyzes data and forwards requests to appropriate NCMEC divisions and departments and monitors online services, news reports, and other sources each day for new cases and information relative to the issues of child sexual exploitation. The ECD also follows up with law enforcement agencies about cases of exploited children.

In addition to the ECD, a separate unit in NCMEC—the Sex Offender Tracking Team within the Case Analysis and Support Division—also works on exploited children's issues. The team provides technical assistance to law enforcement tracking noncompliant sexual offenders pursuant to its authorization.

The Child Victim Identification Program (CVIP)

CVIP formally began in 2002 in response to the decision in *Ashcroft v. Free Speech Coalition* (2002), in which the Supreme Court held that federal laws prohibiting pornography are enforceable when they involve identified children, and not images that appear to be children.[49] CVIP analysts assist law enforcement officers and prosecutors with child pornography cases throughout the country using their knowledge of child pornography series as well as the Child Recognition and Identification System (CRIS), NCMEC's proprietary software. Federal, state, and local law enforcement agencies may submit seized images to federal law enforcement agents detailed to NCMEC and request that CVIP examine the images. CVIP analysts use CRIS and visual analysis to determine whether any of the images contain identified child victims. NCMEC maintains information about law enforcement agencies who identified these child victims. CVIP analysts then provide the submitting agencies with contact information for the officers who identified each child victim. Through the end of FY2012, CVIP was aware of 4,822 child victims who were identified by law enforcement agencies around the world.[50]

In April 2007, NCMEC made available a secure website (the Victim Identification Lab) to law enforcement officers and prosecutors to examine sanitized images that contain clues about a child's whereabouts. Authorized users can examine the images and post comments and suggestions for both NCMEC and other authorized users to read. Viable clues or suggestions are pursued by NCMEC in collaboration with local and state law enforcement.

CyberTipline

As discussed above, the CyberTipline began in March 1998 to serve 24 hours a day, seven days a week as the national clearinghouse for tips and leads about child sexual exploitation.[51] The law does not specify that a particular individual make such reports, although it does require that an electronic communication service or a remote commuting service provider (collectively known as electronic service providers or ESPs) make reports of online incidents involving child pornography.[52] The tipline enables ESPs and members of the public to report under eight

---

[49] For further information about *Ashcroft v. Free Speech Coalition* (2002), see CRS Report 95-406, *Child Pornography: Constitutional Principles and Federal Statutes*, by Henry Cohen.

[50] NCMEC, *NCMEC Quarterly Progress Report: July 1-September 30, 2012*, p. 27.

[51] NCMEC's role as administrator of the CyberTipline was authorized by the Prosecutorial Remedies and Other Tools to End the Exploitation of Children Today (PROTECT) Act of 2003 (P.L. 108-21).

[52] ESPs are required to report apparent child pornography to the CyberTipline pursuant to the PROTECT Our Children Act of 2008 (P.L. 110-401). According to NCMEC, 927 of the more than 7,000 estimated ESPs in the United States (continued...)

---

categories: (1) possession, manufacture, and distribution of child pornography; (2) online enticement of children for sexual acts; (3) child prostitution; (4) child sex tourism; (5) child sexual molestation (not in the family); (6) unsolicited obscene material sent to a child; (7) misleading domain names; and (8) misleading words or digital images on the Internet.[53]

Although the CyberTipline began operating in March 1998, NCMEC's role as administrator of the tipline was formally authorized by the Prosecutorial Remedies and Other Tools to End the Exploitation of Children Today (PROTECT) Act of 2003 (P.L. 108-21). The authorizing statute for the MEC program states that the CyberTipline is intended to take reports of "Internet-related child sexual exploitation," but in practice, such incidents do not have to be facilitated by the Internet.[54]

Analysts from NCMEC review reports to the CyberTipline and each report is assigned a priority level of 1, 2, or 3. Reports that are categorized as a "1" are given the highest priority and indicate that a child is in imminent danger. In evaluating the reports, analysts may, among other things, (1) determine whether an alleged child pornography image is that of an actual child; (2) determine whether an image and content in a report is new or has been viewed by law enforcement in the past; or (3) gather information from open source online sources (e.g., email addresses, websites, and other information) to learn more about the perpetrator and victim.[55] NCMEC analysts then select a "reclassified incident type" based on 19 reclassified incident types.[56]

Regardless of how a report is classified, NCMEC makes reports to the CyberTipline (along with accompanying analysis) available to select federal, state, and local law enforcement agencies through a secure web-based system. Certain federal law enforcement agencies have access to all reports: the Federal Bureau of Investigation (FBI), U.S. Immigrations & Customs Enforcement (ICE),[57] U.S. Postal Inspection Service (USPIS), the Military Criminal Investigative Organizations (MCIO), and the Child Exploitation and Obscenity Section (CEOS) within the Justice Department's Criminal Division.[58] These users are able to access all CyberTipline reports

---

(...continued)

had complied with the law requiring ESPs to report child pornography to the tipline as of September 30, 2012. NCMEC, *NCMEC Quarterly Progress Report for July 1-September 30, 2012*, p. 29.

[53] The first three reporting categories were specified in P.L. 108-21, and the other five categories were specified in the Protecting Our Children Comes First Act of 2007 (P.L. 110-240).

[54] Based on correspondence with the National Center for Missing and Exploited Children, November 2011. See also, NCMEC, CyberTipline, "Watch the CyberTipline Video," http://www.missingkids.com/missingkids/servlet/PageServlet?LanguageCountry=en_US&PageId=2447.

[55] U.S. Government Accountability Office, *Combating Child Pornography: Steps are Needed to Ensure That Tips to Law Enforcement are Useful and Forensic Examinations are Cost Effective*, GAO-11-334, March 2011, p. 9, http://www.gao.gov/new.items/d11334.pdf. (Hereinafter, U.S. Government Accountability Office, *Combating Child Pornography*.)

[56] NCMEC analysts reclassify each report under 19 categories, including—child pornography (confirmed), child pornography (not Internet-related); child pornography (unconfirmed); child pornography (unconfirmed—international); child prostitution; child sex tourism; child sexual molestation; child trafficking (nonsexual exploitation); cyberbullying; online enticement – pretravel; online enticement – travel; other type of incident; appears to be adult; not enough info/dummy record; auto-referral international; and anime/drawing/virtual; SPAM; unable to access; and ESP test report.

[57] ICE forwards reports that involve perpetrators and victims outside of the U.S. to relevant foreign law enforcement agencies.

[58] NCMEC refers reports of misleading domain names and unsolicited materials sent to children to the Department of Justice's Child Exploitation and Obscenity Section in the Criminal Division.

---

ever submitted, and they may search for and select reports by incident type. Analysts forward reports to local or state law enforcement agencies, via the ICAC task forces, when they can identify the geographic location of a suspect, the victim, or both. The ICAC task forces are only able to access reports that are within their respective jurisdictions. The secure system logs every report opened by each agency, and each federal agency has the ability to indicate if they plan to take further action on a particular report.[59] According to NCMEC, what constitutes an "action" taken varies across law enforcement agencies. NCMEC requests feedback from all agencies about the status of reports; however, these agencies do not always indicate whether they have taken action or what resulted from their investigations.

Sex Offender Tracking Team

The Adam Walsh Child Protection and Safety Act of 2006 (P.L. 109-248) expanded the requirements for state law enforcement and prison officials to track and register sex offenders. In partnership with the U.S. Marshals Service (USMS), NCMEC's Sex Offender Tracking Team, in its Case Analysis Division, serves as the central information and analysis hub and assists in efforts to apprehend non-compliant registered sex offenders. Analysts support the USMS, Federal Bureau of Investigation, state sex offender registries, and other state and local law enforcement nationwide to assist in identifying and locating non-compliant registered sex offenders.

The team developed a standard protocol in response to law enforcement requests for assistance in locating fugitive sex offenders, which generally includes information obtained through public databases and search tools routinely used by NCMEC analysts.

Family Advocacy Services

NCMEC's Family Advocacy Division provides support, crisis-intervention, and technical assistance to families, law enforcement, and family-advocacy agencies. Team HOPE (Help Offering Parents Empowerment), a component of the division, consists of trained volunteers who have experienced the disappearance of a child in their family. These volunteers mentor other parents and families of missing children to help them cope during and after a missing incident.

The Family Advocacy Division also collaborates with the 36 American and Canadian missing children advocacy groups that collectively form the Association of Missing and Exploited Children's Organizations (AMECO), by providing technical assistance (such as training sessions on working with law enforcement and identifying the needs of victims) and hosting site visits to NCMEC. AMECO is funded through the MEC program, as discussed below.

Training and Technical Assistance

NCMEC trainers provide on- and off-site training and technical assistance to law enforcement, criminal and juvenile justice professionals, and healthcare professionals nationwide and in Canada. Training involves issues relating to child sexual exploitation and missing-child case detection, identification of victims, investigation, prevention, and forensic imaging. NCMEC provides nationally accredited training about infant security for healthcare professionals,

---

[59] GAO, *Combating Child Pornography*.

including nursing and security personnel. In FY2011, NCMEC trained 8,981 professionals on these issues. NCMEC provides nationally accredited training about infant security for healthcare professionals, including nursing and security personnel.

Partnerships

Work with Federal Agencies

As discussed above, NCMEC works closely with federal agencies, some of which have detailed agents and analysts to work at NCMEC part-time or full-time. These analysts follow CyberTipline leads and work with NCMEC to develop policy and procedures around children missing internationally, among other activities.

Work with State Clearinghouses

Each state, the District of Columbia, Puerto Rico, the U.S. Virgin Islands, and Canada have devoted resources to missing and exploited children's activities through clearinghouses located within law enforcement agencies.[60] These clearinghouses disseminate information and collect data about missing individuals, provide technical assistance in cases of missing and exploited children, and network with other clearinghouses. NCMEC provides the clearinghouses with training, technical assistance, and information to assist them in handling missing-children cases.

Public-Private Partnerships

NCMEC coordinates public and private programs seeking to locate, recover, or reunite missing children with their legal custodians; identify ways to expand and enhance current programs; and help promote the development, advancement, and sponsorship of NCMEC programs. NCMEC staff members create partnerships and maintain relationships with nonprofit and corporate partners to create a network for NCMEC programs.[61]

Background Screening Pilot Program

The PROTECT Act created a pilot program to screen employees and volunteers at three children organizations: Boys & Girls Clubs of America, the National Mentor Partnership, and National Council of Youth.[62] The program has been extended six times, most recently through March 2012 by P.L. 111-341. NCMEC did not receive appropriations for this pilot program through the MEC

---

[60] For further information, see NCMEC, *Missing-Child Clearinghouse Program*, http://www.missingkids.com/ missingkids/servlet/ServiceServlet?LanguageCountry=en_US&PageId=1421.

[61] A list of community supporters and corporate sponsors is available online at http://www.missingkids.com/ missingkids/servlet/PageServlet?LanguageCountry=en_US&PageId=2296.

[62] 42 U.S.C. §5119(a). The most recent amendment to the PROTECT Act (P.L. 111-341) authorizes NCMEC to provide background checks to any nonprofit organization that provides "care"—with approval by NCMEC and in accordance with the FBI—as that term is defined in §5 of the National Child Protection Act of 1993, codified at 42 U.S.C. §5119(c). "Care" is defined as "the provision of care, treatment, education, training, instruction, supervision, or recreation to children, the elderly, or individuals with disabilities." NCMEC provided background checks to multiple child-serving organizations since the creation of the pilot program.

program or any funding source. NCMEC discontinued the program in March 2011 due primarily to a lack of funding.[63]

Over the course of the pilot program, NCMEC processed 104,954 records for prospective volunteers at child-serving nonprofit organizations. Of these records, 1,914 (1.8 %) received a "red light," meaning the applicant had a conviction for a criterion offense (any felony or misdemeanor offense not included on the list of non-serious offenses published periodically by the FBI), or the applicant was on a sex offender registry. Another 4,592 (4.4%) of applicants received a "yellow light," meaning that they were arrested for a criterion offense, but case results were not available.[64]

Financial Coalition Against Child Pornography

In 2006, NCMEC and the International Centre for Missing and Exploited Children joined with 29 international financial institutions and Internet industry leaders to combat commercial online child pornography. The purpose of the coalition is to prevent the purchase and sale of child pornography over the Internet and to engage in prevention efforts. NCMEC, law enforcement agencies, and financial institutions share information pertaining to commercial child pornography websites with the goal of eliminating the ability for users to pay for access to these websites.

Community Outreach

NCMEC works with community partners to prevent incidents of missing and exploited children. The "Hand in Hand with Children: Guiding and Protecting" campaign is an initiative to educate families about keeping children safer. NCMEC's External Affairs Division (EAD) staff work with mayors and state officials to hold child safety events to stress the importance of child protection measures. EAD is also responsible for other community outreach activities. The division uses staff and volunteers from around the country to attend school meetings and conferences about child safety. EAD manages the Campaign Against Sexual Exploitation (CASE) to engage large urban communities in protecting children from becoming victims of sexual exploitation.

NetSmartz Workshop is an online resource guide (www.NetSmartz.org) for children ages 5 to 17, parents, law enforcement, and educators to keep children safer online and empower children to make safer decisions about their Internet use. The website includes English- and Spanish-language brochures on the program and resources, such as Blog Beware, to alert children and their parents of the possible dangers of social networking sites. NetSmartz staff members also train educators and law enforcement about the resources available through NetSmartz.

Finally, the Minority Outreach Program provides information to minority communities to make them aware that minority children are overrepresented among the missing children population. The goals of the program are to educate families about measures to help keep children safer from individuals who seek to harm children, to help families respond in the event a child becomes missing, and to assist families with recognizing symptoms in suspected cases of sexual exploitation.

---

[63] Letter from Ernie Allen, Chief Executive Officer of NCMEC, to Senators Hatch and Schumer, March 4, 2011. Letter provided to CRS by NCMEC.

[64] NCMEC, *NCMEC Quarterly Progress Reports for March 1-June 30, 2011.*

Internet Crimes Against Children (ICAC) Task Force

The Internet Crimes Against Children (ICAC) Task Force program was first funded in 1998 under appropriations law (Justice Appropriations Act, P.L. 105-119) to provide federal support for state and local law enforcement agencies to combat online enticement of children and the proliferation of pornography. Subsequent appropriation laws also provided funding. The PROTECT Our Children Act of 2008 (P.L. 110-401) formally authorized the program. P.L. 110-401 provides two authorizations for the ICAC Task Force program—one for $60 million for FY2009-FY2013 for ICAC activities generally, including grants for ICAC task forces, and one for $2 million for each of FY2009-FY2016 for the National ICAC Data System, a data system to facilitate online law enforcement investigations of child exploitation. The Child Protection Act of 2012 (P.L. 112-206), signed into law on December 7, 2012, authorizes appropriations of $60 million for ICAC activities through FY2018.

ICAC Task Forces

As outlined in the law, some of the purposes of the task forces are as follows: (1) increasing the investigative capabilities of state and local law enforcement officers in the detection, investigation, and apprehension of Internet crimes against children offenses or offenders, including technology-facilitated child exploitation offenses; (2) conducting proactive and reactive Internet crimes against children investigations; (3) providing training and technical assistance to ICAC task forces and other law enforcement agencies in the areas of investigations, forensics, prosecution, community outreach, and capacity-building, using recognized experts to assist in the development and delivery of training programs; (4) increasing the number of Internet crimes against children offenses being investigated and prosecuted; and (5) developing and delivering Internet crimes against children public awareness and prevention programs, among other purposes.

An ICAC task force is formed when a state or local law enforcement agency enters into a grant contract with OJJDP, and then into a memorandum of understanding with other federal, state, and local agencies. Currently, 61 regional task forces have been created, each of which are comprised of multiple affiliated organizations (most of which are city and county law enforcement agencies).[65] All states have a regional task force or belong to a task force in a neighboring state.[66] Efforts are underway to expand ICACs to Indian country.[67] The task forces receive leads from CyberTipline analysts at NCMEC and concerned citizens or develop leads through proactive investigations and undercover operations. P.L. 110-401 authorizes the Attorney General to award

---

[65] U.S. Department of Justice, *The National Strategy for Child Exploitation Prevention and Interdiction: A Report to Congress*, August 2010, p. 58, http://www.justice.gov/ag/defendingchildhood/resources.html. (Hereinafter, U.S. Department of Justice, *The National Strategy for Child Exploitation Prevention and Interdiction: A Report to Congress*.)

[66] U.S. Department of Justice, Office of Justice Programs, "Department Of Justice Announces Internet Crimes Against Children Task Forces In All 50 States," press release, October 15, 2007, http://www.usdoj.gov/opa/pr/2007/October/07_ojp_061.html.

[67] U.S. Department of Justice, Office of Justice Programs, Office of Juvenile Justice and Delinquency Prevention, *FY 2010 Child Protection Programs in Tribal Communities*, http://www.ojjdp.gov/grants/solicitations/FY2010/CPPTribal.pdf. Fox Valley Technical College was awarded a grant to undertake these efforts, http://www.ojp.usdoj.gov/pfig?OCOM_SOL_TITLE_STATE&P_FISCAL_YEAR=2010&P_SOL_TITLE=OJJDP%20FY%2010%20Child%20Protection%20Programs%20In%20Indian%20Country.

grants to state and local ICAC task forces using a formula established by DOJ to distribute 75% of the funds; and the remaining 25% of the funds are to be distributed based on need. In establishing any formula, the law directs DOJ to ensure that each state or local ICAC task force shall, at a minimum, receive an amount equal to 0.5% of the funds available. In addition, DOJ is to take into consideration factors such as each state's population; the number of investigative leads within the task force's jurisdiction; the number of criminal cases related to Internet crimes against children referred to a task force for federal, state, or local prosecution; the number of successful prosecutions of child exploitation cases by a task force; the amount of training, technical assistance, and public education or outreach by a task force on child exploitation offenses; and other criteria established by DOJ to demonstrate the level of need for additional resources.

ICAC Task Force members currently receive training and technical assistance at courses through Fox Valley Technical College (FVTC) of Appleton, WI. Since 1998, FVTC, in partnership with NCMEC and OJJDP, has trained law enforcement officials, state and local government agencies, child protection staff, and others on responding to missing and exploited children's cases. The PROTECT Act further enables the Attorney General to establish national training programs to support the mission of the program.

National ICAC Data System (NIDS)

P.L. 110-401 directs the Attorney General to establish the National ICAC Data System (NIDS). As discussed in the law, the intent of Congress in authorizing the data system was to build upon Operation Fairplay developed by the Wyoming Attorney General's office. Operation Fairplay established a secure, dynamic undercover infrastructure that has facilitated online law enforcement investigations of child exploitation, information sharing, and the capacity to collect and aggregate data on the extent of the problems of child exploitation.[68] The data system is to be housed and maintained within DOJ or a credentialed law enforcement agency and is to be available for a nominal charge to support law enforcement agencies' efforts to combat child exploitation. It must also collect and report real time data, provide an undercover infrastructure for users, identify high-priority suspects, and include a network that provides for secure, online data storage and analysis, among other items. P.L. 112-206, enacted on December 7, 2012, requires that the Attorney General submit a report to Congress on the status of the establishment of the system within 90 days of the law's enactment.

As discussed in a March 2011 GAO report on federal efforts to combat child pornography, DOJ issued a grant solicitation in March 2009 for constructing, maintaining, and housing NIDS; however, grant applicants were notified in January 2010 that DOJ would not make an award under that solicitation and instead would pursue a different system for "deconfliction" and investigation than was described in the solicitation.[69] DOJ issued another solicitation in June 2010 to select a grantee to conduct a national needs assessment and perform other tasks to support the future development of NIDS. In September 2010, OJJDP awarded a grant to the Massachusetts State Police and its partners to conduct a national needs assessment for the National Internet Crimes Against Children Data System (NIDS).[70] As part of this assessment, the Massachusetts

---

[68] For further information, see http://www.usatoday.com/news/nation/2008-04-15-childporn-side_N.htm.

[69] GAO, *Combating Child Pornography*.

[70] U.S. Department of Justice, Office of Justice Programs, *Needs Assessment and Development Activities for the National Internet Crimes Against Children Data System (NIDS)*, http://www.ojjdp.gov/grants/solicitations/FY2010/ (continued...)

State Police is evaluating technical resources, such as software programs and investigative tools, that can be used as building blocks for NIDS; developing new software programs or investigative tools that are needed in undercover investigative work; and conducting research activities to assist DOJ in implementing the ICAC-related requirements of the PROTECT Act.[71] According to DOJ, NIDS will not be developed until after the completion of the national needs assessment.[72]

National Strategy for Child Exploitation Prevention and Interdiction

P.L. 110-401 directed the Attorney General to create and implement a National Strategy for Child Exploitation Prevention and Interdiction. The strategy was to involve establishing long-range, comprehensive goals for child exploitation and for DOJ to coordinate its programs to combat child exploitation with other federal programs, as well as with international, state, local, and tribal law enforcement agencies and the private sector. As part of this strategy, DOJ was directed to assess the ICAC program, including an evaluation of how entities that comprise each task force coordinate on investigations and the success of task forces at leveraging state and local resources and matching funds. The law also directed the Attorney General to conduct periodic reviews of the effectiveness of each ICAC task force. The act requires DOJ to submit a report on the strategy to Congress every other year.

In August 2010, the Department of Justice submitted its first report on the national strategy to Congress, which included information about the ICAC Task Force program.[73] According to the report, the overall goal of the strategy is to prevent child sexual exploitation from occurring in the first place. The report explained that the federal government is coordinating internally and with social service providers, educators, non-governmental organizations, caregivers, and others to meet this goal. The report provides an assessment of the threat to children based on four types of child sexual exploitation: (1) child pornography, (2) online enticement of children for sexual purposes, (3) commercial sexual exploitation of children (primarily domestic prostitution), and (4) child sex tourism. According to the report, cases of child sexual exploitation have increased

---

(...continued)

ARRA%20NIDS.pdf.

[71] Separately, DOJ is funding the ICAC Deconfliction System (IDS), which is a system to be used by ICAC task forces that will replace a previous system, known as the ICAC Data Network. When NIDS is completed, the two systems will be linked so that IDS can facilitate deconfliction among law enforcement agencies that use NIDS. U.S. Department of Justice, Office of Justice Programs, Office of Juvenile Justice and Delinquency Prevention, *FY 2011 Internet Crimes Against Children Deconfliction System Program*, http://www.ojjdp.gov/grants/solicitations/FY2011/ICACIDS.pdf. The grant announcement does not explicitly define "deconfliction;" however, this term is defined by the U.S. Government Accountability Office, in the context of investigations of pornography via the Internet, as "the coordination and information sharing among law enforcement agencies on multijurisdiction investigations to help ensure officer safety and the effective use of resources." U.S. Government Accountability Office, *Combating Child Pornography*, p. 4.

[72] This information was provided to the Congressional Research Service by the U.S. Department of Justice, Office of Justice Programs, in March 2011 and January 2012.

[73] U.S. Department of Justice, *The National Strategy for Child Exploitation and Prevention: A Report to Congress*, August 2010, http://www.justice.gov/psc/docs/natstrategyreport.pdf. This report provides a detailed overview of the ICAC program, including the number of investigations of alleged child sexual victimization, arrests made as a result of those investigations, criminal referrals to the U.S. Attorneys for prosecution, forensic examinations, real children who were victims of some form of abuse, trained ICAC personnel at each task force, and other information; information on training for ICAC personnel; the number and location of ICAC task forces; and federal funding of each task force, among other information.

---

dramatically across all four areas. The report goes on to provide detailed information about the efforts of the various agencies (the Departments of Defense, Health and Human Services, Homeland Security, Justice, Labor, and State; and the U.S. Postal Service) and organizations, including NCMEC, to combat child sexual exploitation. In each of the four areas listed above (as well as child exploitation in Indian country), the strategy emphasizes certain priorities. For example, in response to the domestic prostitution of children, the Department of Justice is exploring whether to expand the FBI's Innocence Lost initiative into other cities and is considering strategies to reduce the demand for prostituted children through public awareness campaigns and enforcement. In addition, DOJ is looking into the ways that the ICAC task force and the Innocence Lost task forces can coordinate further.

P.L. 110-401 additionally directs DOJ to appoint a senior official to serve as coordinator of the national strategy. DOJ appointed the National Coordinator in January 2010. Soon thereafter, the national coordinator convened the National Strategy Working Group to assist in implementing the national strategy.[74] Members of the group include participants from multiple federal agencies and five ICAC Task Forces. The Working Group is comprised of subcommittees that address implementation of specific provisions of the strategy, including technical assistance, global outreach, community outreach, research and grant planning, training, and law enforcement collaboration.

AMBER Alert Program

AMBER (America's Missing: Broadcast Emergency Response) Alert systems are state administered. The MEC program supports these programs by providing training and technical assistance to law enforcement personnel and AMBER Alert administrators. AMBER systems are voluntary partnerships—between law enforcement agencies, broadcasters, and transportation agencies—to activate messages in a targeted area when a child is abducted and believed to be in grave danger. The first system began locally in 1996 when fourth-grader Amber Hagerman was abducted and murdered near her home in the Dallas-Fort Worth area. After the abduction, law enforcement agencies in North Texas and the Dallas-Fort Worth Association of Radio Managers developed a plan to send out an emergency alert about a missing child to the public through the Emergency Alert System (EAS), which interrupts broadcasting.[75] Soon after, jurisdictions in Texas and other states began to create regional alert programs.

Program Administration

The PROTECT Act (P.L. 108-21) authorized the Attorney General to create a national AMBER Alert program to eliminate gaps among state, local, and interstate AMBER Alert networks. The act provided that the Attorney General appoint an AMBER Alert coordinator to (1) work with states to encourage the development of additional regional and local AMBER Alert plans; (2) serve as the regional coordinator of abducted children throughout the AMBER Alert network; (3) create voluntary standards for the issuance of alerts, including minimum standards that addressed the special needs of the child (such as health care needs) and limit the alerts to a geographical

---

[74] U.S. Government Accountability Office, *Combating Child Pornography*, pp. 12-13.

[75] For further discussion about the distribution of the alerts, see CRS Report RS21453, *Amber Alert Program Technology*, by Linda K. Moore.

area most likely to facilitate the abduction of the child, without interfering with the current system of voluntary coordination between local broadcasters and law enforcement; (4) submit a report to Congress by March 1, 2005, on the activities of the Coordinator and the effectiveness and status of the AMBER plans of each state that has implemented such a plan; and (5) consult with the FBI and cooperate with the Federal Communications Commission in implementing the program.

In 2003, the DOJ AMBER Alert coordinator was appointed and convened a national advisory group to oversee the national initiative and make recommendations on the AMBER Alert criteria, examine new technologies, identify best practices, and identify issues with implementation. On the basis of the group's recommendations, the department issued guidelines for issuing an alert: law enforcement officials have a reasonable belief that an abduction has occurred; law enforcement officials believe that the child is in imminent danger of serious bodily injury or death; enough descriptive information exists about the victim and the abductor for law enforcement to issue an alert; the victim is age 17 or younger; and the child's name and other critical data elements have been entered into the National Crime Information Center (NCIC) system. A new AMBER Alert "flag" was created within NCIC for abducted children for whom an alert has been issued. The department submitted a report to Congress in July 2005 that provided an overview of its strategy to facilitate a national AMBER Alert plan and the criteria developed to issue an alert.[76]

DOJ Grant

DOJ's Office of Justice Programs first provided funding for local and state AMBER Alert programs in 2002, with $10 million in discretionary funding. Authority to federally fund these programs through DOJ (and the Department of Transportation, see below) was formalized under the PROTECT Act (P.L. 108-21). P.L. 108-21 authorizes DOJ to provide grants to states, on a geographically equitable basis as possible, to develop and enhance their AMBER Alert communications plans. The law authorizes $4 million for FY2004 for this purpose. Congress has continued to provide funding in each year since FY2004. DOJ has not used the funds for AMBER Alert systems, and instead has determined that funds would be most efficiently spent delivering consistent, comprehensive training and technical assistance to states.[77]

DOT Grant

The PROTECT Act also authorized (and Congress subsequently appropriated) $20 million through the Department of Transportation (DOT) for states to develop and enhance communications systems along highways for alerts and other information for the recovery of abducted children. States are eligible to receive funding (up to $400,000 each, from the one-time appropriation of $20 million)—to be used for the *implementation* of a communications program that employs changeable message signs or other motorist information systems—if DOT determines that the state has already developed the program.[78] At the end of FY2010 (October 31,

---

[76] U.S. Department of Justice, Office of Justice Programs, *Report to the Congress on AMBER Alert*, July 2005, p. 7, http://www.amberalert.gov/newsroom/pdfs/05_amber_report.pdf. (Hereinafter referred to as U.S. Department of Justice, *Report to Congress on AMBER Alert*).

[77] This information was provided to the Congressional Research Service by the U.S. Department of Justice, Office of Justice Programs in May 2007.

[78] Pursuant to the PROTECT Act, states are eligible to receive two types of DOT grants. *Development* grants to be used (continued...)

2010), 40 states and the District of Columbia received funding. The federal share of the cost of these activities is not to exceed 80%, and federal funds are available until expended.[79] Approximately $4.1 million in funding was still available at the end of FY2012.

AMBER Alert Training and Technical Assistance

Every five years OJJDP issues a competitive solicitation seeking bids to provide technical training for law enforcement around techniques to recover missing and exploited children. Funding for this bid was awarded most recently as a five-year cooperative agreement beginning with FY2010. Fox Valley Technical College was awarded the bid and provides training and technical assistance for multiple courses on child abduction and related courses.[80]

At the request of the Department of Justice, NCMEC serves as the national clearinghouse for AMBER Alert information and employs a full-time AMBER Alert law enforcement liaison. NCMEC verifies AMBER Alerts and disseminates information about an abduction to authorized secondary distributors that can target messages to their customers in a specific geographic region. (Only law enforcement can initiate and release AMBER Alerts for primary distribution.) In May 2005, DOJ and NCMEC partnered with CTIA-The Wireless Association to encourage customers to sign up to receive wireless AMBER Alerts on their cell phones.[81] NCMEC partners with 82 secondary distributors, including wireless providers who encourage customers to sign up to receive wireless AMBER Alerts on their cell phones.[82]

Other Program Activities

The MEC program provides funding to support other activities related to missing and exploited children, including program administration, support services provided by missing children's organizations, and grant programs that can vary from year to year.

OJJDP provides training and technical assistance on missing and exploited children for public and private nonprofit organizations,[83] and funds the development and printing of publications and Missing Children's Day activities through DOJ's National Criminal Justice Reference Service.

(...continued)

to develop general policies, procedures, training, and communication systems for changeable message signs or other motorist information about an abduction. Implementation grants are to be used to support the infrastructure of the program. Funding authorized under the PROTECT Act was used exclusively for the *implementation* of communication systems to issue AMBER alerts. However, states are eligible to apply for grants up to $125,000 each, through a separate DOT appropriation for the Intelligent Transportation Systems program, to support state departments of transportation efforts related to AMBER Alert planning. These funds are available until expended.

[79] This information was provided to the Congressional Research Service by Department of Transportation, Federal Highway Administration staff in January 2013.

[80] U.S. Department of Justice, "AMBER Alert Program, Technical Assistance," http://www.amber-net.org/technicalassistance.html.

[81] U.S. Department of Justice, *Report to Congress on AMBER Alert*, p. 7.

[82] NCMEC, *NCMEC Quarterly Progress Reports for July 1-September 30, 2012*, p. 18.

[83] For further information, see U.S. Department of Justice, Office of Justice Programs, Office of Juvenile Justice and Delinquency Prevention, "Missing and Exploited Children's Program Training and Technical Assistance," http://mecptraining.org/.

The program also provides a grant to the National Alliance of Missing Children's Organizations (NAMCO). NAMCO is a membership organization of nonprofit organizations that serve the families of missing and exploited children, provide services to law enforcement and community agencies, and provide public awareness and education about child protection.

Other program activities vary each year. DOJ funded the following grants through the MEC program in recent years:

- Child Protection Research: This FY2011 grant funded research on missing and exploited children and on how technology facilitates crimes against children, including identifying predictive factors that reliably indicate whether a subject of an online child exploitation investigation poses a great risk of harming children.

- Technical Assistance to Programs to Address Commercial Sexual Exploitation (CSE)/Domestic Minor Sex Trafficking (DMST): This FY2011 grant funded an organization to provide technical assistance to OJJDP grantees and other organizations addressing CSE or DMST of girls and boys. The program offers education and training, expert consultations, peer-to-peer networking opportunities, resources, and other tailored assistance to respond to diverse communities concerning the sexual victimization of girls and boys.

- Youth with Sexual Behavior Problem: The purpose of this FY2010 program was to assist localities in responding to child sexual victimization by youth. The organizations were directed to provide intervention and support services for the offending youth and treatment services for the victims and their families.

- Improving Community Response to the Commercial Sexual Exploitation of Children (CSEC): The purpose of this program, from FY2009, was to support three communities in combating the commercial sexual exploitation of children, which includes youth under age 18, by improving training and coordination activities within the community. OJJDP assisted the communities in developing policies and procedures to identify CSEC victims, adopting best practices for addressing CSEC, and completing a needs assessment to identify and fill gaps in local service provision to victims, such as mental and physical health services and temporary shelter.

- Research on the Commercial Sexual Exploitation of Children: The purpose of this FY2009 program was to support research on the scope and consequence of the commercial sexual exploitation of children and youth.

- Promoting Child and Youth Safety—Community Initiatives and Public Awareness: The purpose of this FY2009 program was twofold: (1) to help communities develop and implement evidence-based demonstration projects that promote child and youth safety and (2) to provide resources and expertise to help communities develop effective public awareness strategies about youth safety.

Issues

Issues that are relevant to the MEC program include the potential need for more comprehensive data on missing and sexually exploited children; the implementation of the National ICAC Data System; and the creation of the National Emergency Child Locator Center at NCMEC that provides assistance to jurisdictions experiencing disasters. Other issues pertain to children missing from foster care and missing adults.

Data Collection

P.L. 110-240 authorizes NCMEC to engage in particular data collection activities. The law permits NCMEC to report to DOJ the number of missing and recovered children but not to engage in data collection other than receiving reports about missing children. Further, P.L. 110-240 authorizes NCMEC to take reports through its CyberTipline of incidents of child exploitation under multiple exploitation categories; NCMEC already took these reports prior to the enactment of P.L. 110-240.

OJJDP has funded two data collection waves since the Missing Children's Assistance Act passed in 1984. The most recent wave, NISMART-2, conducted in 1999 (discussed above), lacks statistics about the number of exploited children, except in the case of nonfamily abductions and runaways (however, the survey did not distinguish between the share of children who ran away because of sexual abuse from those who experienced physical abuse, and it did not report the share of children who experienced both forms of abuse). Further, due to the limited number of nonfamily abductions each year, the estimates of caretaker missing and reported missing cases are imprecise.[84] Limited data for all types of missing episodes also precluded NISMART-2 from drawing conclusions about episode types by region.

In FY2010, DOJ awarded funds for a follow-up study known as NISMART-3. As with NISMART-2, NISMART-3 will include several complementary studies to measure the size and nature of the missing children problem.[85] The studies will provide national estimates of missing children based on surveys of households, juvenile residential facilities, and law enforcement agencies.

A related issue concerns requirements about entering data of missing children, including young adults ages 18 to 21, into the federal National Crime Information Center (NCIC) Missing Person File. As discussed above, the NCIC is a computerized index of information on crimes and criminals that is maintained by the FBI. Under federal law, (1) no law enforcement agency within a state may establish or maintain policies that require a waiting period before accepting a missing child or unidentified person report; (2) no law enforcement agency may establish or maintain any policy that requires the removal of a missing person entry from NCIC (or the state law enforcement system) solely based on the age of the person; and (3) the report of each missing child must include certain items, such as demographic information, location of the last known contact with the child, and the category under which the child is reported. States must further ensure that law enforcement agencies enter the profile of each child—including young adults ages 18 to 21—to the NCIC (and state law enforcement database) within two hours of receiving a report that he or she is missing.[86]

---

[84] Finkelhor, Hammer, Sedlak, *Nonfamily Abducted Children*, p. 7. See discussion of NISMART-2 earlier in this report for explanation of "caretaker missing" and "reported missing" cases.

[85] U.S. Department of Justice, Office of Justice Programs, Office of Juvenile Justice and Delinquency Prevention, Grant Solicitation, *OJJDP FY 2010 National Incidence Studies of Missing, Abducted, Runaway, and Thrownaway Children 3*, 2010, http://ojjdp.ncjrs.gov/grants/solicitations/FY2010/NISMART3.pdf.

[86] The National Child Search Assistance Act of 1990 (P.L. 101-647) required law enforcement agencies to enter these profiles "immediately." The Adam Walsh Child Protection and Safety Act (P.L. 109-248) struck "immediately" and (continued...)

In a 2011 study, the Government Accountability Office (GAO) reported that across 10 states, reports of missing children to NCIC were untimely in 9% to 47% of cases in each of the states.[87] GAO also reviewed steps that the FBI has taken to ensure implementation of the two-hour entry rule and documented challenges with meeting the requirements for entry into NCIC, as reported by nine law enforcement agencies. Such challenges included determining whether a child is missing when the child is involved in disputes over custody, and obtaining information about children missing from foster care. GAO found that while the FBI has tried to mitigate these challenges, the agency should consider establishing minimum standards for states to monitor compliance with these requirements and to obtain and share information about improving compliance.[88]

National ICAC Data System

As discussed above, DOJ is in the process of developing the NIDS, which began with an assessment of how best to create and maintain the system. DOJ has reported multiple obstacles for creating NDIS. For example, DOJ must ensure NIDS is accessible by multiple entities (the ICAC task forces and federal, state, local, and tribal law enforcement officials); however, the systems these entities use may not be compatible. Still, DOJ believes that the system will be implemented.[89] Given some of these initial challenges, Congress may want to monitor its implementation.

National Emergency Child Locator Center

P.L. 110-240 specifies that MEC funds may be used to operate the National Emergency Child Locator Center (NECLC). The law also adds as a purpose of the MEC program that it helps children who go missing because of natural disasters such as hurricanes and floods.

During the evacuations of Hurricanes Katrina and Rita in 2005, thousands of children were separated from their parents and sent to different emergency shelters. NCMEC was asked by DOJ to lead federal and local efforts to recover missing children. As part of its response, NCMEC created a special Katrina/Rita hotline and mobilized Team Adam personnel to locate and reunite all missing and dislocated children (over 5,000) with their families.[90] Recognizing the need for formalized coordination efforts in disasters or emergencies, Congress passed legislation (P.L. 109-295) requiring FEMA to establish the National Emergency Child Locator Center (NECLC)

(...continued)

replaced it with "within two hours." Suzanne's Law (part of the PROTECT Act of 2003, P.L. 108-21) directs law enforcement agencies to also submit, within the same two-hour time frame, information about missing adults ages 18 through 20 to the NCIC.

[87] For most of these reports, the law enforcement agencies could not provide the reason why they were untimely. When reasons were provided, law enforcement most often reported that they were unaware of the two-hour requirement or that they did not provide information about the child in a timely matter for a variety of reasons (i.e., they began investigating the case before submitting the report, were dispatched to another service call before submitting the report, or did not think the report was necessary because it involved a child who was a frequent runaway).

[88] U.S. Government Accountability Office, *Missing Children; DOJ Could Enhance Oversight to Help Ensure That Law Enforcement Agencies Report Cases in a Timely Manner*, GAO-11-444, June 2011, http://www.gao.gov/products/GAO-11-444.

[89] GAO, *Combating Child Pornography*. pp. 32-33.

[90] National Center for Missing and Exploited Children, *Annual Report 2005*, pp. 5-7.

within NCMEC. The law also required that the FEMA Administrator establish procedures so that all relevant information about displaced children will be made immediately available to NCMEC. In 2011, FEMA and NCMEC signed an agreement formally establishing the NECLC; however, NCMEC already had in place a Disaster Response Plan (DRP) describing how the organization would respond to disasters.[91] The DRP was created in 2007 and updated in 2011.[92] The plan details the response to a continuum of disaster types. For example, NCMEC would operate its hotline 24 hours a day, seven days a week to respond to questions from law enforcement and other emergency officials for a Level 1 disaster (a local man-made or natural disaster, such as a fire). A Level 4 disaster (a catastrophic event declared by the President, such as Hurricane Katrina) would warrant NCMEC deploying Team Adam staff in the field to shelters established in a multi-state region.

NCMEC continues to work on the implementation of the NECLC and has assisted communities affected by disasters. According to NCMEC, the NECLC consists of operational components as well as physical components, including facilities, equipment, and a computer network. The physical components are housed at a backup Call Center in NCMEC's Lake Park, FL, facility.

Child Welfare Disaster Planning

The NECLC does not appear to address children missing from foster care due to a disaster, though the federal government has recently issued guidelines regarding how state child welfare systems should respond to disasters.

During the Gulf Coast hurricanes, thousands of children in foster care were forced to evacuate their homes. Almost 2,000 of Louisiana's 5,000 foster children were displaced by the hurricanes, and nearly one out of five displaced foster children left the state.[93] The state's child welfare system had difficulty tracking the children during and after the hurricanes. Foster parents knew to call the child welfare agency, but social workers' phones were not operational for weeks following Hurricane Katrina. Louisiana officials experienced difficulty contacting the children because case information was not in a central database and more than 300 current records were destroyed. At the time, there were no federal requirements to develop child welfare disaster plans, and only 20 states and D.C. had a written plan (Louisiana and Mississippi were among the states that lacked a plan).[94] Of those plans, 19 addressed preserving child welfare records, 13 addressed identifying children who might be dispersed, and 10 addressed coordination with other states.

In August 2006, Congress passed P.L. 109-288 to amend the Child Welfare Services program (Title IV-B, Subpart 1 of the Social Security Act), requiring that states develop procedures, no later than September 29, 2007, to respond to and maintain child welfare services in the wake of a disaster. The act specified that HHS establish criteria for how state child welfare systems would respond. These criteria include (1) identify, locate, and continue services for children under the care or supervision of the state and who are displaced or adversely affected by the disaster; (2) respond appropriately to new child welfare cases in areas adversely affected by a disaster and

---

[91] This information was provided by NCMEC in April 2007.

[92] Ibid, January 2012.

[93] U.S. Government Accountability Office, *Lessons Learned for Protecting and Educating Children after the Gulf Coast Hurricanes*, GAO-06-680R, May 2006, p. 3.

[94] U.S. Government Accountability Office, *Child Welfare: Federal Action Needed to Ensure States Have Plans to Safeguard Children in the Child Welfare System Displaced by Disasters*, GAO-06-944, July 2006, p. 2.

provide services in those cases; (3) remain in communication with caseworkers and other essential child welfare personnel displaced because of a disaster; (4) preserve essential program records; and (5) coordinate services and share information with other states.[95] States are required to submit, in their child welfare plan (known as the Child and Family Services Plan),[96] procedures describing how the state would respond to a disaster based on the five criteria above. HHS has also updated its 1995 guide to assist child welfare agencies develop disaster relief plans.[97]

Children Missing from Foster Care[98]

The Missing Children's Assistance Act does not include provisions for children missing from foster care; however, media attention to the case of Rilya Wilson, a six-year-old foster child missing from the Florida child welfare system and presumed to have been murdered, has raised concerns about Florida and other states'[99] ability to track children in the foster care system and ensure their safety while under the custody of the child welfare agency.

A child is considered missing from foster care if she or he is not in the physical custody of the child welfare agency or the institution or person with whom the child has been placed, due to (1) the child leaving voluntarily without permission (i.e., runaways); (2) the family or nonfamily member removing the child, either voluntarily or involuntarily, without permission (i.e., abductions); or (3) a lack of oversight by the child welfare agency.[100] The majority of children known to be missing from foster care are runaways. According to the U.S. Department of Health and Human Services, on the last day of FY2011, nearly 6,000 (1%) of the 400,540 children in foster care had run away. For that same year, approximately 1,400 (1%) of the 245,260 children who exited foster care exited as runaways.[101] However, these figures do not convey the total number of children who go missing.[102] Kids can go missing for a variety of reasons, including abduction or benign circumstances, such as misunderstandings about a schedule.

---

[95] 42 U.S.C. §622(b)(16).

[96] To receive federal funding, state child welfare agencies must submit annually its procedures for carrying out the federal Child Welfare Services program.

[97] Mary O'Brien, Sarah Webster, and Angela Herrick, *Coping with Disasters and Strengthening Systems: A Framework for Child Welfare Agencies,* University of Southern Maine, Edmund S. Muskie School of Public Service, February 2007, available online at http://muskie.usm.maine.edu/helpkids/rcpdfs/copingwithdisasters.pdf.

[98] For further information, see Congressional Research Service Congressional Distribution memo, *Children Missing From Foster Care: Background, Responses by Select States, and Issues,* by Adrienne L. Fernandes-Alcantara. Available upon request.

[99] Megan O'Matz and Sally Krestin, "States Share DCF's Woes; Caseworkers Elsewhere Often Unable to Find Missing Children," *Sun-Sentinel,* September 15, 2002, p. 1A.

[100] Caren Kaplan, *Children Missing from Care,* Child Welfare League of America, 2004, http://www.cwla.org/programs/fostercare/childmiss.htm. (Hereinafter referred to as Kaplan, *Children Missing from Care.*)

[101] U.S. Department of Health and Human Services, Administration for Children and Families, *The AFCARS Report #19, Preliminary FY 2011 Estimates as of July 2012,* http://www.acf.hhs.gov/sites/default/files/cb/afcarsreport19.pdf. For additional information about runaway youth, see CRS Report RL33785, *Runaway and Homeless Youth: Demographics and Programs,* by Adrienne L. Fernandes-Alcantara.

[102] Some states and counties have calculated the number of missing foster children under their care, based on jurisdiction-specific definitions. After the Rilya Wilson incident, Florida determined that 393 children were missing from care, of whom 339 (86.3%) had run away and 31 (7.9%) were parentally abducted. A small share (4.8%) of children were endangered, meaning that they were missing under circumstances that put them in physical danger, such as a predatory abduction or kidnapping.

No federal laws specifically address the issue of children missing from foster care. However, Titles IV-B and IV-E of the Social Security Act require state child welfare agencies to monitor and provide for the safety and well-being of children in out-of-home foster care.[103] Under Section 471 (Title IV-E), states are eligible for federal foster care maintenance payments if, among other requirements, they develop a case plan (as defined under Section 475, which also applies to Title IV-B) for each child that details the type of home or institution in which the child is placed. The case plan must discuss the safety and appropriateness of the placement and a plan for assuring that the child receives safe and proper care.

States must also develop a system (as defined under Section 475) to review, no less than every six months, the status of the child's case plan. Also, under Section 471, states must check child abuse and neglect registries (including federal crime databases) for criminal information about prospective and current foster parents. Finally, under Section 424 (Title IV-B), states must ensure that children in foster care are visited by their caseworkers on a monthly basis and that the majority of the visits occur in the child's residence. Section 424 sets forth a penalty structure for violating these and other requirements.

In response to the Rilya Wilson case, the Child Welfare League (CWLA), a child advocacy organization, in partnership with NCMEC, created the Children Missing from Care Project in 2004. Drawing on the expertise of policy makers, child welfare advocates, and law enforcement officials, the CWLA and NCMEC developed best practices guidelines around missing foster children.[104] The guidelines provide a framework for collaboration between the law enforcement agency and the child welfare agency. They recommend that the two share a uniform definition of missing children (based on the three criteria outlined above) and a clear delineation of shared and distinct roles. Child welfare agencies and law enforcement officials are encouraged to receive cross-training and to create an integrated local information system about children.

The guidelines provide guidance to child welfare agencies to prevent missing-from-care episodes, including quality supervision; training stakeholders about risk factors for running away; and frequent contacts between case workers and children, caregivers, and birth families. To respond effectively to missing episodes, the guidelines recommend that child welfare agencies provide accurate and up-to-date records with information about the child and a management information system to track information related to missing episodes.

Missing Adults[105]

NCMEC provides services for missing young adults ages 18 to 20, pursuant to Suzanne's Law, which was passed as part of the PROTECT Act.[106] This law amended the Missing Children's

---

[103] Titles IV-B and IV-E and related sections of the Social Security Act are compiled at http://www.acf.hhs.gov/ programs/cb/resource/safe2010draft. See also 42 U.S.C. §§620-629(i), 670-679(b).

[104] Child Welfare League of America, *CWLA Best Practice Guidelines: Children Missing From Care*, 2005 and National Center for Missing and Exploited Children, *Children Missing From Care: The Law enforcement Response*, 2005. The NCMEC publication is available at http://www.missingkids.com/missingkids/servlet/ResourceServlet? LanguageCountry=en_US&PageId=2234.

[105] For additional information, see CRS Report RL34616, *Missing Adults: Background, Federal Programs, and Issues for Congress*, by Adrienne L. Fernandes-Alcantara; and CRS Report R40552, *Alert Systems for Missing Adults in Eleven States: Background and Issues for Congress*, by Adrienne L. Fernandes-Alcantara and Kirsten J. Colello.

[106] Suzanne's Law was passed as part of the PROTECT Act (P.L. 108-21). It raised the age of missing children reported to the FBI's National Crime Information Center from age 17 to age 20. 42 U.S.C. §5779(a).

Assistance Act by requiring law enforcement agencies to enter individuals under the age of 21 into the NCIC.[107] NCMEC processes young adult cases differently than cases for missing children. NCMEC will accept a young adult case only if it is reported by a law enforcement officer—and not by parents, spouses, partners, or others—because NCMEC relies on the officer to verify that the young adult is missing due to foul play or other reasons that would cause concern about the individual's whereabouts (e.g., diminished mental capacity). Once individuals reach the age of majority, they may have legitimate reasons for becoming missing, such as seeking protection from a domestic abuser.

---

[107] No corresponding amendments to the Missing Children's Assistance Act have been made to reflect that NCMEC is authorized to accept cases of missing children ages 18 to 20.

Appendix A. Demographics of Missing and Exploited Children

This appendix provides additional information about demographics of missing and exploited children, including definitions of missing children, characteristics of missing children episodes, and the number of children sexually abused or at risk of sexual exploitation.

Definitions of Missing Children

NISMART-2 classified missing children under five categories. **Figure A-1** defines these five categories.

Figure A-1. Categories of Missing Children

> **Non-family Abduction:** A non-family member takes a child (without lawful authority or parental permission) by physical force or threat of bodily harm or keeps a child by force in an isolated location for at least an hour; or when a child 14 years or younger (or who is mentally incompetent) is taken (without lawful authority or parental permission), detained, or voluntarily accompanies a nonfamily perpetrator who conceals the child's whereabouts, asks for ransom, or plans to keep the child permanently. A type of non-family abduction, known as a **stereotypical kidnapping** involves detaining the child overnight, transporting him or her at least 50 miles, and holding the child for ransom with the intent of keeping the child permanently or of killing the child.

> **Family Abduction:** A member of a child's family or someone acting on behalf of a family member, violates a custody order, decree, or other legal custodial rights, by taking or failing to return the child and conceals or transports the child out of state with the intent of preventing contact or depriving the caretaker of custodial rights indefinitely or permanently. There must be evidence that a child 15 years or older (unless mentally incompetent) was taken or detained by physical force or was threatened with bodily harm.

> **Runaway/Thrownaway:** A runaway is a child who either leaves home and stays away overnight without parental permission; is 14 years or younger (or older if mentally incompetent) who leaves home, chooses not to return and stays away overnight; or is 15 years or older who leaves home, chooses not to return and stays away two nights. A thrownaway child is one who is asked or told to leave the home by a parent or other adult in the household who has not made adequate alternative care arrangements for the child, and the child is away from home overnight; or a child who leaves home, but is prevented from returning by a parent or other household adult who has not arranged adequate alternative care for the child who is away from home overnight.

> **Missing Involuntary, Lost, or Injured:** A child's whereabouts are unknown to the caretaker, which causes the caretaker to become alarmed for at least one hour while trying to locate the child under one of two conditions: (1) the child is trying to get home and contacts the caretaker, but is unable to do so because the child is either lost, stranded, or injured; or (2) the child is too young to know how to return home or contact the caretaker.

> **Missing Benign Explanation:** A child's whereabouts are unknown to the caretaker, which causes the caretaker to (1) be alarmed, (2) try to find the child, and (3) call the police about the situation for any reason, as long as the child was not lost, injured, abducted, victimized, or considered to be a runaway or thrownaway.

Source: Congressional Research Service presentation of definitions in Sedlak et al., *National Estimates of Missing Children: An Overview*, U.S. Department of Justice, Office of Juvenile Justice and Delinquency Prevention, October 2002, p. 4.

Incidents of Missing and Non-Missing Children

Some children in NISMART-2 were not counted as missing (i.e., "non-missing" children) because their short-term or long-term missing incident failed to alarm their caretakers and/or prompt their caretakers to report them as missing. Such cases included runaway or thrownaway children who went to the home of a relative or friend, causing their caretakers little or no concern; children held by family members in known locations, such as the home of an ex-spouse; and children abducted by nonfamily but released before anyone noticed their absence. **Table A-1** includes the missing and non-missing children within each category. Note that estimates of these children are not totaled across categories because some children had more than one type of missing episode. The researchers caution against summing the categories of missing children because these categories contain multiple (not individual) counts.

Table A-1. Missing and Non-missing Children

Missing Category	Missing	Non-missing
Nonfamily abduction	33,000	25,200
Family abduction	117,200	86,700
Runaway/thrownaway	628,900	1,054,000
Missing involuntarily, lost, or injured[a]	198,300	0
Missing benign explanation[a]	374,700	0

Source: Congressional Research Service presentation of data from Andrea J. Sedlak et al., *National Estimates of Missing Children: An Overview*, U.S. Department of Justice, Office of Juvenile Justice and Delinquency Prevention, October 2002, p. 10.

a. By definition, all children with these episodes are known to be missing.

Characteristics of Missing Children

Runaway and Thrownaway Children

The majority of runaway and thrownaway children in the NISMART-2 study were between the ages of 15 and 17 (68% of all cases), followed by children ages 12 and 14.[108] An equal number of boys and girls experienced runaway or thrownaway incidents. White children made up the largest share of runaways (57%), followed by black children (17%) and Hispanic children (15%). Over half of all children left home for one to six days, and 30% traveled approximately one to 10 miles. An additional 31% traveled more than 10 to 50 miles. Nearly all (99%) runaway and thrownaway children were returned to their homes. Based on 17 indicators of harm or potential risk measured in NISMART-2, 71% of the surveyed children were placed at risk for harm when they were away from home.[109] The survey found that 17% of runaway children used hard drugs and 18% were in the company of someone known to be abusing drugs when they were away from home. Other risk factors included spending time in a place where criminal activity was known to occur (12%),

---

[108] Hammer, Finkelhor, and Sedlak, *Runaway/Thrownaway Children*.

[109] Jan Moore, *Unaccompanied and Homeless Children Review of Literature (1995-2005)*, National Center for Homeless Education, 2005, p. 6, http://www.cde.state.co.us/cdeprevention/download/pdf/ Homeless%20Youth%20Review%20of%20Literature.pdf.

---

involvement with a violent person (7%), and physical assault or attempted physical assault by another person (4%).

In other studies of runaways and thrownaways, children most often cite family conflict as the major reason for leaving home or being forced to leave home.[110] A child's relationship with a step-parent, sexual activity, sexual orientation, pregnancy, school problems, and alcohol and drug use are strong predictors of family discord. Over 20% of children in NISMART-2 reported being physically or sexually abused at home in the prior year or feared abuse upon returning home.

Children Missing Involuntarily or for Benign Reasons

Children can become missing involuntarily as a result of being lost or sustaining an injury that prevents them from returning home or to their caretaker, such as a broken leg or a fall that renders them unconscious. Benign circumstances such as miscommunication among family members can also cause a child to be considered missing by their caretakers. NISMART-2 found that most children missing involuntarily or for benign reasons were white, male, and older. They disappeared most frequently in wooded areas or parks and were most often gone for one hour to six hours (77% of all cases). In most cases, their caretakers knew they were missing because they disappeared from their supervision (39%) or failed to return home (29%).

Nonfamily Abductions

The experiences of children abducted by strangers, slight acquaintances, or others (i.e., friends, babysitters) often involved detention in an isolated place through the use of physical force or threat of bodily harm. More serious abduction cases—known as stereotypical kidnappings—may also include detaining the child overnight and transporting them outside of their community, with the intent to keep the child permanently or kill the child. Extensive media coverage about stereotypical kidnapping cases may contribute to the belief that these missing children incidents are common. However, such cases are rare; about 115 (90 of whom were caretaker/reported missing) of the estimated 58,200 victims of nonfamily abductions in 1999 experienced a stereotypical kidnapping.[111]

With the caveat that NISMART-2 data on nonfamily abductions are not entirely reliable because some estimates are based on too few sample cases, the most frequent victims of both broadly defined nonfamily abductions and stereotypical nonfamily abductions were teenage girls ages 12 to 14.[112] Approximately 60% of all victims, male and female, were abducted by male acquaintances or strangers. Streets (32% of all cases), parks or wooded areas (25%), and other

---

[110] For additional information, see CRS Report RL33785, *Runaway and Homeless Youth: Demographics and Programs*, by Adrienne L. Fernandes-Alcantara.

[111] David Finkelhor, Heather Hammer, and Andrea J. Sedlak, *Nonfamily Abducted Children: National Estimates and Characteristics*, U.S. Department of Justice, Office of Justice Programs, Office of Juvenile Justice and Delinquency Prevention, October 2002, p. 6, http://www.ncjrs.gov/pdffiles1/ojjdp/196467.pdf.

[112] Estimates of nonfamily abductions are based on the combination of data collected in the NISMART-2 Household Surveys and the Law Enforcement Study. The Household Surveys, in which adults and children were interviewed by phone, provide data on broadly defined nonfamily abductions. These surveys are limited because they may have undercounted children who experienced episodes but were living in households without telephones or were not living in households during the study period. Children who were reported as victims in both the adult and children interviews were counted only once in the unified estimate. The Law Enforcement Study yielded data on stereotypical kidnappings.

---

public places (14%) were places from which children were typically abducted, and children who were moved, were taken into vehicles (45%) or to the perpetrator's home (28%). In nearly half of all broadly defined and stereotypical kidnapping incidents, the perpetrator sexually assaulted the child, and in a third of the cases, the perpetrator physically assaulted the child. Less than one percent of children missing due to a nonfamily abduction failed to return home alive.

Family Abductions

Approximately 63% of children abducted by family members were with the abductor under lawful circumstances directly prior to the incident.[113] In these cases, disputes between family members about custodial rights and privileges may have triggered the abduction. Perpetrators most often were the child's father (53% of all cases), followed by the mother (25%) and other relatives.[114] Most children were abducted from their own home or someone else's home, and nearly all the episodes did not involve the use of threat or force. Children age 11 and under and children not living with both parents appeared to be the most likely victims of parental abduction. Almost half of children abducted by family members were returned to the primary caretaker in one week or less, and the majority were returned within one month.

International Family Abductions

NISMART-2 does not track the number of international family abductions; however, a 1998 survey of nearly 100 left-behind parents by the American Bar Association Center on Children and the Law, in collaboration with three missing children's organizations, provides some insight into the characteristics of international abductions by family members.[115] Nearly half of the abductions occurred during a court-ordered visitation by the abducting parent and child. Gender of the child did not appear to be a factor in the abduction, but abducted children tended to be young, with a median age of five years old. In approximately 70% of the cases, the responding parents reported that the child had been located, and 25% said they always knew their child's precise location. About 40% of the parents reported that their child had been recovered by the time of the survey. In half of the cases in which the child was recovered, the separation lasted one year, compared to five years for half the cases in which the child was not recovered.

Incidents of Child Sexual Exploitation

As discussed above, the true number of sexual exploitation incidents, whether or not they accompany missing children cases, is not known because the abuse often goes undetected.

---

[113] Estimates for family abductions are based on data collected in the NISMART-2 Household Surveys. Respondents to family abduction questions were (1) mainly female caretakers of children and (2) generally was the aggrieved caretaker who provided all of the information regarding custodial rights to determine whether a family abduction had occurred. NISMART-2 researchers did not attempt to verify respondent statements.

[114] Heather Hammer, David Finkelhor, and Andrea J. Sedlak, *Children Abducted by Family Members: National Estimates and Characteristics*, U.S. Department of Justice, Office of Justice Programs, Office of Juvenile Justice and Delinquency Prevention, October 2002, http://www.ncjrs.gov/pdffiles1/ojjdp/196466.pdf.

[115] Janet Chiancone, Linda Girdner, and Patricia Hoff, *Issues in Resolving Cases of International Child Abduction by Parents*, U.S. Department of Justice, Office of Justice Programs, Office of Juvenile Justice and Delinquency Prevention, December 2001, http://www.ncjrs.gov/pdffiles1/ojjdp/190105.pdf. (Hereinafter U.S. Department of Justice, *International Child Abduction by Parents*.)

Nonetheless, some studies—in addition to those discussed above—provide insight into the prevalence of sexual exploitation.

Sexual Victimization Among Children Generally

The FBI's National Incident-Based Reporting System (NIBRS) includes data on each single incident of select crimes that are collected by federal, state, and local law enforcement agencies. The data encompass sexual offenses, including forcible rape, forcible sodomy, sexual assault with an object, forcible fondling, incest, and statutory rape. An analysis of 418,000 victims reported by 22 states to NIBRS from 2000 and 2001 found that over half of the crimes committed against juveniles involved sexual assaults.[116] Sexual assaults accounted for three in four juvenile female victims and one in four male victims. Females were more likely to be victimized in their teen years compared to males, who were more likely to be victimized as young children. A limitation of these data is that victims tend to underreport sexual victimization to law enforcement and other agencies.

Sexual Victimization Among Children in the Child Welfare System

Incidents of child abuse—including sexual abuse—and neglect by a caretaker that are reported to the state child welfare system may lead to the removal of a child from his or her home. Two studies track the share of children each year who enter foster care as a result of sexual abuse by their caretaker or family member. The National Child Abuse and Neglect Data System (NCANDS), administered by the U.S. Department of Health and Human Services, provides case-level data on all children under age 18 who received an investigation or assessment by a state child protective services agency. NCANDS is not a nationally representative sample because states are not required to report data, though the majority of states have provided data since CY2000 (beginning in 2002, NCANDS began to collect data on a federal fiscal year basis). Sexual abuse is defined differently across states, but generally includes acts of rape, sexual assault, indecent exposure, as well as facilitating prostitution and creating and distributing pornography.[117] The FY2010 NCANDS report estimated that 9.2% of children, or 63,527, in the child welfare system were victims of sexual abuse during that year.[118]

Using NCANDS data from 1990 to 2000, researchers found a decline in the number of sexual abuse cases, from an estimated 150,000 cases to 89,500 cases.[119] Researchers have concluded that multiple factors likely contributed to the downward trend, and that one of those factors was

---

[116] U.S. Department of Justice, Office of Justice Programs, Office of Juvenile Justice and Delinquency Prevention, *Juvenile Offenders and Victims: 2006 National Report*, pp. 31-32, http://ojjdp.ncjrs.gov/ojstatbb/nr2006/downloads/NR2006.pdf.

[117] U.S. Department of Health and Human Services, *Abuse and Neglect*.

[118] U.S. Department of Health and Human Services, Administration for Children and Families, *Child Maltreatment 2010*, p.47, http://www.acf.hhs.gov/programs/cb/pubs/cm10/cm10.pdf#page=61. Each state defines the types of child abuse and neglect in state statute and policy; however, in exchange for federal funding, each state must include a minimum definition of "child abuse" that is included in the Child Abuse Reporting and Treatment Act (CAPTA). This definition includes the term "sexual abuse," defined in CAPTA (§111(4)) to include "(A) the employment, use, persuasion, inducement, enticement, or coercion, of any child to engage in, or assist any other person to engage in, any sexually explicit conduct or simulation of such conduct for the purpose of producing a visual depiction of such conduct; or (B) the rape, and in the cases of caretaker or inter-familiar relationships, statutory rape molestation, prostitution, or other forms of sexual exploitation of children, or incest with children."

[119] David Finkelhor and Lisa M. Jones, *Explanation for the Decline in Child Sexual Abuse Cases*.

---

probably a true decline in the occurrence of sexual abuse.[120] A true decline in the number of sexual abuse cases is substantiated by a decrease of 56% from 1993 to 2000 in self-reported measures of sexual assault and sexual abuse by children ages 12 to 17 in the National Crime Victimization Survey, conducted annually by the Census Bureau.[121] This decline was due primarily to the decrease in the number of offenses committed by a family member or acquaintance.

Another analysis of children who had contact with child welfare services provides nationally representative data of the characteristics and functioning of children, including rates of sexual victimization. Known as the National Survey of Child and Adolescent Well-Being (NSCAW), the study found in its second wave of data collection (October 1999 through December 2000) that 11% of cases of suspected child abuse included sexual abuse.[122] Sexual abuse was defined along a continuum, which included fondling/molestation (without genital contact) or other less severe types (e.g., exposure to sex or pornography), masturbation, digital penetration of sexual organs, oral copulation (of adult or child), and intercourse. Molestation accounted for just over one-half (55%) of all cases, followed by intercourse (11.4%), digital penetration of sexual organs (11.4%), oral copulation (9.4%), and masturbation (5.2%). The second wave of NSCAW (with data collection from March 2008 to September 2009) found that 8.4% of cases of suspected child abuse included sexual abuse.[123]

Online Victimization of Children

A true estimate of the number of children sexually exploited over the Internet is unknown. The Youth Internet Safety Survey conducted in March to June 2005 by the University of New Hampshire's Crimes Against Children Research Center (commissioned by NCMEC and supported by OJJDP) found that children using the Internet are vulnerable to unwanted sexual solicitation, unwanted exposure to sexual material, and harassment (these categories do not necessarily reflect incidents of child sexual exploitation).[124]

---

[120] Other factors may include decline in the number of self-reports of sexual abuse by victims; decline in related social problems; greater decline in the most readily preventable cases of sexual abuse; and increase in the incarceration of offenders. For further discussion see, Ibid, p. 8.

[121] Ibid, pp. 8-9.

[122] U.S. Department of Health and Human Services, Administration for Children and Families, *National Survey of Child and Adolescent Well-Being (NSCAW): CPS Sample Component Wave 1 Data Analysis Report*, April 2005, http://www.acf.hhs.gov/programs/opre/abuse_neglect/nscaw/. NSCAW provides information about the characteristics of children and families who came into contact with the child welfare system through an investigation by child protective services. The sample includes children whose cases were closed after the investigation, and who remained at home; those who remained at home, but had a case opened to child welfare services, and those who were removed from their homes as a result of the investigation.

[123] U.S. Department of Health and Human Services, Administration for Children and Families, *National Survey of Child and Adolescent Well-Being (NSCAW) II Baseline Report: Maltreatment, Final Report*, August 2011, http://www.acf.hhs.gov/programs/opre/abuse_neglect/nscaw/.

[124] Janice Wolak, Kimberly Mitchell, and David Finkelhor, *Online Victimization of Youth: Five Years Later*, National Center for Missing and Exploited Children, 2006, http://www.unh.edu/ccrc/pdf/CV138.pdf. *Unwanted sexual solicitation* is defined by the study as a request to engage in sexual acts or sexual activities or give personal sexual information that were unwanted, or whether unwanted or not, were made by an adult; *unwanted exposure to sexual materials* refers to a child being exposed to pictures of nude people or people having sex, when conducting online searches, surfing the web, or using e-mail and instant messaging; and *harassment* refers to threats or other offensive behavior (not sexual solicitation) sent online to the child or posted online about the child for others to see.

The share of children exposed to sexual material and solicited online was greater in 2005 than in the previous survey conducted in August 1999 to February 2000. Despite increased use of filtering, blocking, and monitoring software in households of children Internet users, in 2005, more than one-third of children Internet users (34%) saw sexual material online they did not want to see in the past year compared to one-quarter (25%) of children surveyed in 1999 and 2000. Online harassment also increased to 9%, from 6%. However, a smaller share of children (13%) received sexual solicitations compared to children in the previous survey (19%).

A series of other studies on online victimization of children—the National Juvenile Online Victimization studies (NJOV)—has been conducted by the University of New Hampshire's Crimes Against Children Research Center. The NJOV-1 and NJOV-2 were completed in 2001 and 2006. Both studies examined trends in the incidence of arrests for child sexual exploitation that was facilitated by computer technology, and described the dynamics of the crimes and the characteristics of offenders and victims. A third study, NJOV-3, is underway.[125] Although the NJOV-3 will build upon the information provided in the first two studies, it differs from the first two in that it will (1) collect data on the prosecution of technology-assisted commercial sexual exploitation crimes, and (2) collect data from law enforcement and prosecutors about cases of "sexting."[126]

Commercial Sexual Exploitation[127]

The commercial sexual exploitation of children refers to acts of prostitution, pornography, sex trafficking, and sex rings for financial gain.[128] Few studies appear to exist that provide the national prevalence and incidence of commercially exploited children. Estimates have been made, however, of the number of children in groups classified as "high-risk" for commercial sexual exploitation. These groups include sexually exploited children not living in their own homes (i.e., runaway, thrownaway, and homeless children); sexually exploited children living in their own homes; other groups of sexually exploited children, including female gang members who have become victims as a result of their gang membership and transgender street children; and U.S. children and children traveling abroad and in the United States for sexual purposes.[129]

---

[125] University of New Hampshire, Crimes Against Children Research Center, http://www.unh.edu/ccrc/internet-crimes/projects.html. The three National Juvenile Online Victimization studies are funded by the Department of Justice, Office of Justice Programs, Office of Juvenile Justice and Delinquency Prevention under the American Recovery and Reinvestment Act (P.L. 111-5).

[126] University of New Hampshire, Crimes Against Children Research Center, http://www.unh.edu/ccrc/pdf/The%20Third%20National%20Juvenile%20Online%20Victimization%20Study_web%20doc.pdf. The Crimes Against Children Research Center defines "sexting" as youth-generated sexual images of juveniles themselves or peers that meet criminal definitions of child pornography and are created, distributed, or possessed by youth. Note that although accounts of "sexting" are being included in the NJOV-3 study, sexting is not conducted online but rather via cellular telephones.

[127] For further information, see CRS Report R41878, *Sex Trafficking of Children in the United States: Overview and Issues for Congress*, by Kristin M. Finklea, Adrienne L. Fernandes-Alcantara, and Alison Siskin.

[128] The United States is viewed as a primary source of child-sex tourists abroad. In a sample of information about foreign child-sex tourists in Southeast Asia, tourists from the United States were the largest group. See Eva J. Klain, *Prostitution of Children and Child-Sex Tourism: An Analysis of Domestic and International Responses*, National Center for Missing and Exploited Children, April 1999, http://www.icmec.org/missingkids/servlet/ResourceServlet?LanguageCountry=en_X1&PageId=2704.

[129] For the methodology of estimates of groups of children, see Richard J. Estes and Neil Alan Weiner, *The Commercial Sexual Exploitation of Children in the U.S., Canada, and Mexico, Executive Summary of the U.S. National Summary*, September 2001, http://www.sp2.upenn.edu/~restes/CSEC_Files/Exec_Sum_020220.pdf.

Appendix B. The Missing Children's Assistance Act of 1984, as Amended

Table B-1. The Missing Children's Assistance Act of 1984 and Amendments to the Act

Year (Public Law)	Legislative Creation and Amendments to the Missing Children's Assistance Act
1984 (P.L. 98-473)	—Defines *missing child* as any individual under age 18 whose whereabouts are unknown to such individual's legal custodian if he or she was removed from control of his or her legal custodian without custodian's consent or the circumstances strongly indicate that such individual is likely to be abused or sexually exploited;
	—Directs OJJDP Administrator to
	(1) facilitate effective coordination among all federally funded programs relating to missing children,
	(2) establish and operate a national toll-free telephone line for individuals to report information regarding the location of any missing child, or other child 13 years old or younger whose whereabouts are unknown,
	(3) establish and operate a national resource center and clearinghouse designed to provide technical assistance to state and local governments and law enforcement agencies, disseminate information about innovative and model missing children's programs, and periodically conduct national incidence studies to determine the number of missing children,
	(4) analyze, compile, publish, and disseminate an annual summary of recently completed research relating to missing children with emphasis on effective models of inter-governmental coordination and effective programs designed to promote community awareness of missing children, among others, and
	(5) prepare an annual comprehensive plan for facilitating cooperation and coordination among all agencies and organizations with responsibilities related to missing children;
	—Authorizes OJJDP Administrator to make grants and enter into contracts for research, demonstration projects, or service programs designed to disseminate information about missing children, locate missing children, and collect information from states or localities on the investigative practices used by law enforcement agencies in missing children's cases, among other purposes; and
	—Provides funding authorization at $10 million for FY1985 and such sums as necessary for FY1986 through FY1988.
1988 (P.L. 100-690)	—Removes the requirement that the OJJDP Administrator analyze, compile, publish, and disseminate an annual summary of recently completed research concerning missing and exploited children;
	—Requires OJJDP Administrator to submit a report, within 180 days after the end of each fiscal year, to the President and Congress, including a comprehensive plan for facilitating cooperation and coordination among all agencies and organizations with responsibilities related to missing children; identify and summarize effective models of cooperation; identify and summarize effective programs for victims of abduction; and describe in detail the activities in the national resource center and clearinghouse, among other requirements;
	—Requires OJJDP Administrator to disseminate information about free or low-cost legal, restaurant, lodging, and transportation services available for the families of missing children, as well as information about the lawful use of school records and birth certificates to identify and locate missing children;
	—Requires OJJDP Administrator to establish annual research, demonstration, and service program priorities for making grants and contracts, and criteria based on merit for making such grants and contracts; limits a grant or contract to $50,000 unless the grant is competitive;
	—Provides funding authorization at such sums as necessary for FY1989 through FY1992.

Year (Public Law)	Legislative Creation and Amendments to the Missing Children's Assistance Act
1989 (P.L. 101-204)	Technical amendments only.
1992 (P.L. 102-586)	Provides funding authorization at such sums as necessary for FY1993 through FY1996.
1994 (P.L. 103-322)	Establishes a task force composed of law enforcement officers from pertinent federal agencies to work with the National Center for Missing and Exploited Children and coordinate federal law enforcement resources to assist state and local authorities in investigating the most difficult cases of missing and exploited children.
1996 (P.L. 104-235)	—Requires that the OJJDP Administrator use only up to 5% of the amount appropriated for a fiscal year to conduct an evaluation of the effectiveness of programs and activities under the Missing Children's Assistance Act; —Provides funding authorization at such sums as necessary for FY1997 through FY2001.
1998 (P.L. 105-314)	Deletes the language to establish a task force composed of law enforcement officers from pertinent federal agencies to work with the National Center for Missing and Exploited Children.
1999 (P.L. 106-71)	—Provides an annual grant to the National Center for Missing and Exploited Children to carry out the activities originally designated to the OJJDP Administrator, including the following: (1) operate the national 24-hour, toll-free telephone line, (2) coordinate the operation of the telephone line with the operation of the Runaway and Homeless Children Program's national communications system, and (3) operate the official national resource center and information clearinghouse for missing and exploited children, among other responsibilities; —Requires the OJJDP Administrator to make grants to or enter into contracts to periodically conduct national incidence studies to determine for a given year the actual number of children reported missing, among other statistics; and —Provides funding authorization for the National Center for Missing and Exploited Children at $10 million for FY2000 through FY2003 and such sums as necessary for the Missing Children's Assistance Act program for these same years.
2003 (P.L. 108-21)	—Provides funding authorization for the National Center for Missing and Exploited Children at $20 million for FY2004 through FY2005; and —Provides that the National Center for Missing and Exploited Children coordinate the operation of a cyber tipline to provide online users an effective means of reporting Internet-related child sexual exploitation in the areas of distribution of child pornography, online enticement of children for sexual acts, and child prostitution.
2003 (P.L. 108-96)	Provides funding authorization for the National Center for Missing and Exploited Children at $20 million for FY2004 through FY2008 and such sums as necessary for the Missing Children's Assistance Act program for these same years.
2006 (P.L. 109-248)	Changes the definition of *missing child* to any individual less than 18 years of age whose whereabouts are unknown to such individual's legal guardian.
2008 (P.L. 110-240)	Provides funding authorization for the National Center for Missing and Exploited Children at $40 million for FY2008 and such sums as necessary for FY2009 through FY2013, and such sums as necessary for the Missing Children's Assistance Act program for these same years. The law also authorizes the OJP Administrator to make the grant to NCMEC to carry out specified activities, some of which were already carried out by the organization before the law was enacted.
2008 (P.L. 110-344)	Provides authority to an Inspector General to authorize staff to assist NCMEC by conducting reviews of inactive case files to develop recommendations for further investigations and by engaging in similar activities.

Source: Compiled by the Congressional Research Service.

Note: The Missing Children's Assistance Act is codified at 42 U.S.C. §5771 et seq.; under Chapter 72 (Juvenile Justice and Delinquency Prevention).This compilation includes only legislation amending the Missing and Exploited Children's program at §5771 et seq. The Internet Crimes Against Children (ICAC) Task Force Program, a component of the Missing and Exploited Children's Program, is authorized under the PROTECT Our Children Act (P.L. 110-401), at 42 U.S.C. §17601 et seq., under Chapter 154 (Combating Child Exploitation). The AMBER Alert program, another component of the Missing and Exploited Children's program, is authorized under the PROTECT Act (P.L. 108-21) and is codified at 42 U.S.C. §5791.

Author Contact Information

Adrienne L. Fernandes-Alcantara
Specialist in Social Policy
afernandes@crs.loc.gov, 7-9005